"Who Do You Say I Am?"

Answers Right From Jesus

John A. Braun

I0805926

NORTHWESTERN PUBLISHING HOUSE
Milwaukee, Wisconsin

All Scripture quotations, unless otherwise indicated, are taken from the Holy Bible, English Standard Version®. ESV®. Copyrighted © by Crossway Bibles, a publishing ministry of Good News Publishers, Wheaton Illinois. Used by permission of Good News Publishers. All rights reserved. The "ESV" and "English Standard Version" trademarks are registered in the United States Patent and Trademark Office by Crossway Bibles. Use of either trademark requires the permission of Crossway Bibles.

All rights reserved. This publication may not be copied, photocopied, reproduced, translated, or converted to any electronic or machine-readable form in whole or in part, except for brief quotations, without prior written approval from the publisher.

Northwestern Publishing House
N16W23379 Stone Ridge Dr., Waukesha WI 53188-1108
www.nph.net
© 2024 Northwestern Publishing House
Published 2024
Printed in the United States of America
ISBN 978-0-8100-3197-5
ISBN 978-0-8100-3198-2 (e-book)

24 25 26 27 28 29 30 31 32 33 10 9 8 7 6 5 4 3 2 1

Contents

Preface

Jesus asked his disciples, "Who do you say that I am?" (Matthew 16:15). His question came just after the Pharisees and Sadducees asked him to show them a sign from heaven. But they were not interested in proof that Jesus was God from above. They only wanted ammunition to accuse him and discredit his message.

Just after Jesus asked his disciples who they thought he was, he showed them an astonishing sign. He was transfigured before Peter, James, and John. God from above, yes. As he talked with the Old Testament prophets Moses and Elijah, the disciples heard a voice proclaim, "This is my beloved Son, with whom I am well pleased; listen to him" (Matthew 17:5).

Anyone who has studied the life of Jesus knows that many believed his claim to be the Son of God. However, the gospel accounts also reveal that many did not. During the last year of his life, he confirmed those who believed and challenged those who did not. That year has been called the year of opposition and serves as a counterpoint to the previous year, the year of popularity.

As I listened to Jesus defend himself before his critics and doubters, I wondered about our world today. Many believe that Jesus is the Son of God come to earth, but many others raise serious objections to his claims. We find ourselves confirming the faith of disciples who confess with Peter that Jesus is "the Christ, the Son of the living God" (Matthew 16:16). But we also find others opposing Jesus' claims with the claims of the critics and doubters.

Jesus certainly taught and confirmed the faithful, but he also was not shy about defending his claims in the face of his enemies. He did that before the Jewish court that condemned him and stood boldly claiming he was superior to Pilate. I do not live in a perfect Christian world. I certainly am not a perfect disciple with all the answers to those who oppose the message of Jesus, but I wondered if I could learn something from Jesus. How did he defend himself and assert the truth? I wondered if another way to look at that last year of his life was to call it the year of apologetics, that is, the year of defense. Calling it the year of opposition puts the focus on the opponents. But the Jesus we see is firm, bold, powerful, and unflinching. He spoke pointedly, proclaiming both law and gospel. Without hiding the truth or seeking a compromise, he was calling even these opponents to realize he was who he claimed to be—"the Son of the living God."

Those thoughts became a wish to sit at the feet of Jesus to listen and learn like his disciples had done to learn how to comfort the believers and defend the truth boldly. Those disciples were with him in both the year of popularity and the times of opposition. Perhaps it was their course on apologetics. They learned how to defend the truth with love for the faithful and their opponents. I simply ask you to take a place at Jesus' feet with me to find confirmation that he is God from above who redeemed us all and to learn from him about defending the truth. Consider these devotions my humble notes as I sat, read, and thought about "the Christ, the Son of the living God."

1

Anointed

Jesus returned in the power of the Spirit to Galilee, and a report about him went out through all the surrounding country. And he taught in their synagogues, being glorified by all. And he came to Nazareth, where he had been brought up. And as was his custom, he went to the synagogue on the Sabbath day, and he stood up to read. "The Spirit of the Lord is upon me, because he has anointed me to proclaim good news to the poor." And he rolled up the scroll and gave it back to the attendant and sat down. And the eyes of all in the synagogue were fixed on him. And he began to say to them, "Today this Scripture has been fulfilled in your hearing." When they heard these things, all in the synagogue were filled with wrath. And they rose up and drove him out of the town and brought him to the brow of the hill on which their town was built, so that they could throw him down the cliff. But passing through their midst, he went away. (Luke 4:14-16,18,20-21,28-30)

John the Baptist had prepared the way for Jesus' appearance. Then Jesus appeared and was baptized in the Jordan River as the Father announced, "This is my beloved Son, with whom I am well pleased" (Matthew 3:17). After his temptation, Jesus returned to Galilee and went to Nazareth, where he had grown up.

In the early days of his ministry in Galilee, the sky was sunny for Jesus. It's not that the weather was always predominantly sunny but that during most of his Galilean ministry, crowds followed him and praised him. He healed many, taught in their synagogues, and even taught large crowds on the hills and along the Sea of Galilee. Few clouds darkened his work. So it is not surprising that news "went out through all the surrounding country."

When he came to the synagogue in Nazareth on the Sabbath, a kind of celebrity excitement filled the air. Here was Jesus the miracle worker! The people expected something more than the regular Sabbath gathering. In the synagogue, Jesus, the hometown hero, stood up to read. One of the leaders handed Jesus the scroll of the prophet Isaiah. Jesus searched the scroll for a particular passage. He could have turned to the references about Galilee: "He has made glorious the way of the sea, the land beyond the Jordan, Galilee of the nations. The people who walked in darkness have seen a great light" (Isaiah 9:1-2). But he was looking for another passage from the great prophet.

Jesus unrolled the scroll until he found the passage he wanted. He read, "The Spirit of the Lord is upon me, because he has anointed me to proclaim good news to the poor" (see Isaiah 61:1). When Jesus had been given the courtesy of addressing those who came to the synagogue, everyone had wondered what he would say. Now they were curious about what he would say about this passage from Isaiah. When he finished reading, he rolled up the scroll, gave it back to the attendant, and sat down. Luke says the eyes of everyone there watched in expectation. Then Jesus said, "Today this Scripture has been fulfilled in your hearing."

The first reaction of the people in the synagogue seemed positive: "All spoke well of him and marveled at the gracious words that were coming from his mouth" (Luke 4:22). They must have sensed that Jesus was claiming to be the Messiah for whom they had been waiting for so long. Yes, Jesus said he was "anointed" to proclaim good news. *Messiah* and the Greek *Christ* mean "anointed." This claim of Jesus did not escape them, and at first they dared to hope that the one before them was that special deliverer. They knew about all he was doing in Galilee. Was he the one who would honor Galilee? Was he the light that had dawned as Isaiah had also foretold (Isaiah 9:1-2)? What amazing news!

Another reaction set in. "Is not this Joseph's son?" (Luke 4:22). Joseph, Mary, and Jesus had settled in Nazareth when the young family returned from Egypt after Herod died. So Joseph the carpenter may have done work for some of these people. Some think that Jesus helped his father as he learned the trade. Others suggest that

Joseph's family became part of the business too. Whatever occurred, these people were familiar with Jesus and his family.

Jesus had just said he was the fulfillment of a prophecy that stretched back seven hundred years. So they wanted some demonstration that this claim of Jesus was more than just a fantastic boast. Jesus understood and said, "Doubtless you will quote to me this proverb, 'Physician, heal yourself.' What we have heard you did at Capernaum, do here in your hometown as well" (Luke 4:23). In other words, "Show us you are the one you claim to be." But Jesus went on: "No prophet is acceptable in his hometown" (Luke 4:24). That set the people off. They wanted to boast about a hometown hero. But his claim bordered on blasphemy and, at best, was an example of arrogant megalomania. Just who did he think he was?

Their disappointment led to rejection and then to furious violence. They drove Jesus out of town to the edge of a hill to throw him down. But he simply walked right through the crowd and went on his way. It was not yet his time. Jesus came not just as a great teacher or even a miracle worker. He was also anointed, designated, and set aside by God's ancient design. "The Spirit of the Lord" was upon him to proclaim good news.

In the months that followed, Jesus would travel through Galilee proclaiming the good news. That's what he was anointed to do. Over time, the opposition to Jesus would grow and became so disruptive that he would leave Galilee and often avoid large crowds. Then he would fulfill his teaching ministry by concentrating on the disciples, often in private, to prepare them for the important task of proclaiming the good news after he ascended. By his grace, we are his disciples now. Proclaiming the good news is our task also. Let us sit quietly and listen to him so that we may treasure his truth more deeply and be better prepared to proclaim the gospel.

PRAYER: Jesus, I have come to know you as the Messiah and my Savior. Some who do not know you belittle you and me because of what I believe. Do not walk away from me when others challenge my faith. Stay with me and give me the strength and the words to confess you as my Savior. Teach me your truth and prepare me to share it. Amen.

2

Lord of the Sabbath

At that time Jesus went through the grainfields on the Sabbath. His disciples were hungry, and they began to pluck heads of grain and to eat. But when the Pharisees saw it, they said to him, "Look, your disciples are doing what is not lawful to do on the Sabbath." He said to them, "Have you not read what David did when he was hungry, and those who were with him: how he entered the house of God and ate the bread of the Presence, which it was not lawful for him to eat nor for those who were with him, but only for the priests? Or have you not read in the Law how on the Sabbath the priests in the temple profane the Sabbath and are guiltless? I tell you, something greater than the temple is here. And if you had known what this means, 'I desire mercy, and not sacrifice,' you would not have condemned the guiltless. For the Son of Man is lord of the Sabbath." (Matthew 12:1-8)

Not everyone became a disciple of Jesus. In Nazareth, some drove him out of town and were ready to throw him off a cliff (Luke 4:14-30). In the synagogue there, Jesus read a passage from Isaiah and claimed to be the Anointed One, the Christ, whom Isaiah had written about. "How could that be?" the people wondered. They knew his family; he was the carpenter's son. He was just like them. But now he was claiming to be so much more. This incident happened at the beginning of Jesus' ministry. He had much more to do before his life was over. So Jesus frustrated his Nazarene opponents and went on his way.

Jesus spent much of the next year in Galilee, where he attracted large crowds of people, healed their diseases, and taught them God's truth. For his chosen disciples, the Twelve, he used this time to draw them closer to him, answering their questions and preparing them to carry on his work without him. The opposition in Nazareth that Luke records did not go away even during the time in Galilee. Discussion about Jesus was part of the daily conversation, and people had differing opinions about him.

The people, especially the Pharisees, watched Jesus and discussed everything he did. Mostly, they were looking for a way to discredit him. On this Sabbath, Jesus was walking through the grainfields and teaching his disciples; the disciples were hungry. They rubbed handfuls of grain to remove the husks and ate the kernels. Snatching handfuls of grain was a common practice. Farmers who planted grain expected travelers to stop at the edge of the field to eat handfuls of grain, much like us stopping for a sandwich. But it was a Sabbath, when the Old Testament laws said they should not work. Technically, they were harvesting and threshing grain.

The opposition that Jesus had encountered in Nazareth took on a different cloak in that grainfield. The Pharisees challenged Jesus and his disciples, accusing Jesus of allowing his disciples to break the Sabbath regulations. And he did!

Jesus' response is striking. First, Jesus cites the example of David and his companions when they were fleeing from Saul and needed food. The only food available was the consecrated bread. That was off-limits to them, reserved for the priests. But in their need, they ate it (1 Samuel 21:1-6). Then Jesus reminded the Pharisees that the priests themselves violate the Sabbath law when they carry out their duties in the temple. Sacrifices, prayers, and official duties did not stop on the Sabbath. The priests worked on the Sabbath to help people worship.

The lesson should have been clear, but Jesus left no doubt. He quoted a passage from the prophet Hosea: "I desire steadfast love and not sacrifice" (Hosea 6:6). The disciples were hungry just as David's men had been hungry. The merciful approach was to give them something to eat even if it meant breaking the ceremonial law.

The second part of Jesus' response raised the stakes. The priests worked in the service of the Lord as they carried out their duties. The disciples were serving the Lord as they listened to and learned from Jesus, the Anointed One. They were excused from Sabbath regulations because of whom they served, just as the priests were excused because they served the Lord. Again, Jesus leaves no doubt about his meaning: "The Son of Man is lord of the Sabbath."

The Pharisees would use this to discredit Jesus. He is Lord of the Sabbath? He has the authority to set aside the ceremonial regulations? They were just teachers of the law, commentators of the Old Testament. But Jesus was more than that. He claimed authority over the Sabbath, not just to be a teacher of the Scriptures. No wonder they opposed him.

What Jesus was asserting here is the same thing he asserted months earlier in Nazareth: He was the Messiah on a mission from God and was more than just a great teacher. He was the Lord. Yet he calls himself "Son of Man," not "Son of God." Understand the dynamics of his mission. Jesus wanted his disciples to see that he was not just a human like them. They had come to listen to his words when John the Baptist pointed to him and said, "Behold, the Lamb of God, who takes away the sin of the world!" (John 1:29). As they followed him and listened, they also watched him perform miracles no human could do. Yes, Jesus was like them, but more. Jesus was helping them grow in that conviction. He wanted their faith to become a conviction that would withstand the opposition after he ascended. In the process, he asserted his authority while keeping his enemies at bay. Later, his parables would be a strategy to both build conviction in his disciples and disarm his opponents.

PRAYER: Jesus, I ask you to deepen my faith in you so that I have a strong conviction that you are my Lord and Savior. Make me sure and strong so that I will not be shaken by those who oppose you and attack my faith in you. Teach me to be ready to share my faith with even those who do not believe and trust in you. Amen.

3

Lawful to Heal on the Sabbath

[Jesus] went on from there and entered their synagogue. And a man was there with a withered hand. And they asked him, "Is it lawful to heal on the Sabbath?"—so that they might accuse him. He said to them, "Which one of you who has a sheep, if it falls into a pit on the Sabbath, will not take hold of it and lift it out? Of how much more value is a man than a sheep! So it is lawful to do good on the Sabbath." Then he said to the man, "Stretch out your hand." And the man stretched it out, and it was restored, healthy like the other. But the Pharisees went out and conspired against him, how to destroy him. (Matthew 12:9-14)

The issue of the Sabbath was not completely settled for the Pharisees. Matthew places this incident in the context of the previous discussion about the Sabbath. Jesus went into their synagogue. Apparently, he was still in Galilee, since Matthew refers to this synagogue as "their" synagogue.

Also, they apparently were not satisfied with the response Jesus had given to their criticism about eating on the Sabbath. Of course, the disciples had not only eaten the grain but also had harvested the kernels and rubbed them with their hands to remove the chaff. But Jesus' response had silenced the Pharisees—at least for a time. But they were still looking for a reason "they might accuse him."

It didn't take long. Jesus knew they were not completely satisfied, and not because his answer in the grainfield about the Sabbath was not thoughtful and on point. They were opposed to Jesus on several levels, and their opposition would erupt in various ways in the next days and months, sometimes over the same issue or some nuance. Here it was focused on the Sabbath laws.

Jesus seized the opportunity to teach and to oppose their scheme to discredit him. In the synagogue that Sabbath, a man with a shriveled hand had come to worship. Jesus used the opportunity to extend the lesson he had taught in the grainfield. There he had focused on the prophet Hosea's words, "I desire steadfast love and not sacrifice" (Hosea 6:6).

Now Jesus echoed that principle with an illustration. "Which one of you who has a sheep, if it falls into a pit on the Sabbath, will not take hold of it and lift it out?" It's common sense that the sheep would need help. Only heartless people would not offer to help that bleating sheep. That's answer enough, but Jesus took one more step that would enflame his opponents rather than satisfy them.

"Of how much more value is a man than a sheep!" he said. He added this lesson: "So it is lawful to do good on the Sabbath." But he didn't stop there. The man in the synagogue with the withered hand is an object lesson. Jesus told the man to stretch out his hand. The man did so in obedience to Jesus' request. What happened next made a deep impression on Matthew and all those who saw it. The man's hand was restored. The Pharisees saw it too, but it confirmed them in their opposition to Jesus. They "went out and conspired against him, how to destroy him."

We sometimes struggle with the chronology of the gospels. Sometimes the sequence of events is clear. At other times, it is not so clear. All the synoptic gospels (Matthew, Mark, and Luke) place this incident, with some variations, early in the story of Jesus' ministry. Luke (6:1-11) and Mark (3:1-6) also record this event. They add a few other details, but the event is essentially the same. This incident may not have occurred in the sequence I have chosen. However, I included it here because of the opposition to Jesus that surfaced early in his ministry.

I've included it for another reason. When Jesus came to Judea nearer the time of his crucifixion, he performed an even more astonishing miracle. He came to Bethany four days after Lazarus had died (John 11). He called Lazarus out of his grave, showing that the power of Jesus was absolute. Even death was no match for him. But the reaction of the Jews was the same as it was in Galilee. They wanted him dead! This opposition seethed in them and was not overcome, not by his words of common sense and mercy or by the power he displayed when he healed this man's hand or when he dried the eyes of the mourning sisters in Bethany by raising their brother.

Understanding the Pharisees, one might easily understand their vehement reaction. It wasn't just that Jesus healed on the Sabbath. It wasn't even that Jesus reminded them to have mercy instead of withholding mercy because of their religious and cultural concerns. He healed! He raised Lazarus! These miracles made it quite clear who Jesus was.

He said that he was Lord of the Sabbath. He had the power to heal. He not only claimed to be God and Lord, but he also had the power to verify his claim and remove all doubt. To the Pharisees, this was blasphemy and called for the harshest punishment the law of God allowed—death.

The rejection of Jesus today follows a similar path. It's not that he just reminds us to show mercy and teaches us who he is. It's that he claimed divine authority. Some opposition today places Jesus with other religious or moral teachers. From that perspective his words are no more important than anyone else's. But no! He is God. Lord of the Sabbath. Lord of all things. His words are more important than anyone else's. More important than mine, yours, or those who still resist his claim that he is God himself.

PRAYER: Lord, you have redeemed me with your precious blood and innocent suffering and death. Your words have assured me of that blessing. Your words have directed me to love others. All too often, Lord, I think my opinion is better than yours, so I make excuses not to listen. Prevent me from excusing myself from what you have taught me as your disciple to think and do. Teach me to remember that your words are truth and power. Mine are weak. As I live for you, fill my heart with deep conviction that you are the Lord of the Sabbath, my Lord, and my Savior. Amen.

4

A Bruised Reed

Jesus, aware of this, withdrew from there. And many followed him, and he healed them all and ordered them not to make him known. This was to fulfill what was spoken by the prophet Isaiah: "Behold, my servant whom I have chosen, my beloved with whom my soul is well pleased. I will put my Spirit upon him, and he will proclaim justice to the Gentiles. He will not quarrel or cry aloud, nor will anyone hear his voice in the streets; a bruised reed he will not break, and a smoldering wick he will not quench, until he brings justice to victory; and in his name the Gentiles will hope." (Matthew 12:15-21)

The plot to kill Jesus was real. Just before Jesus withdrew, he had two disagreements with the Pharisees. First, his disciples had picked grain while walking through a field—an act of harvesting and, therefore, working on the Sabbath. Perhaps the Pharisees remembered the man who had picked up sticks on the Sabbath and was stoned for breaking the Sabbath (Numbers 15:32-42). Jesus had defended his disciples and cited references from the Old Testament as well as his claim that "something greater than the temple is here" (Matthew 12:6).

Then he went to the synagogue and healed a man with a withered hand. He knew the Pharisees were looking to bring charges against him, so he challenged them—"Is it lawful to heal on the Sabbath?" (Matthew 12:10). Then he healed the man in the synagogue on the Sabbath. This event sent the Pharisees over the edge. They "went out and conspired against him, how to destroy him" (Matthew 12:14).

The confrontation clearly pitted two sides against each other—Jesus and the Pharisees. But Jesus did not allow it to become an ugly and pointless shouting match. Jesus withdrew from the synagogue. Isaiah 42:14 (quoted in Matthew 12:18-21) captures the way Jesus approached opposition, even from those who wanted him dead.

He was the Messiah foretold in the Old Testament—chosen and loved by his heavenly Father. The Father had spoken at his baptism and would speak again at the transfiguration: "This is my beloved Son, with whom I am well pleased" (Matthew 3:17). Jesus was sent to proclaim God's truth to all humanity, Pharisees included. A confrontation like this could escalate with both sides shouting slogans and calling names.

Isaiah wrote, "He will not cry aloud or lift up his voice, or make it heard in the street" (Isaiah 42:2). On this Sabbath, Jesus answered the question of the Pharisees clearly and forcefully but without anger or shouting. Then he challenged them by showing mercy to someone in need of healing. What could they say? Jesus had shown restraint while clearly making his point.

As we travel with Jesus during this year of opposition, we will note this principle again and again. He spoke clearly and pointedly, but he did not quarrel or raise his voice in the streets to subdue his opponents. He spoke in a loud voice twice at the Feast of Booths (John 7:28-37)—once to proclaim, "If anyone thirsts, let him come to me and drink" (John 7:37)—and again at the tomb of Lazarus when he called, "Lazarus, come out" (John 11:43). But most often, Jesus spoke with restraint, even when he announced woes on the Pharisees and teachers of the law.

Jesus' restraint was a lesson the disciples needed to see in action. James and John were identified as "Sons of Thunder" (Mark 3:17). When messengers Jesus had sent ahead on a trip to Samaria returned with the news that a Samaritan village would not welcome him, James and John were true to their name "Sons of Thunder." They asked Jesus, "Lord, do you want us to tell fire to come down from heaven and consume them?" (Luke 9:54). They had not learned the lesson and needed the rebuke of Jesus before they moved on to another village.

We are not so different from James and John. Our natural inclination is to get angry and shout when confronted with opposition to our opinions and ideas. We become even more emotionally involved when our dearest and most precious ideas about Jesus are dismissed or we are belittled as ignorant believers in Jesus. Those who oppose us may even resort to bullying us with the opinions of experts claiming that everyone agrees with them. We may have thought something similar to what James and John wanted to do. But heed the lesson of Jesus: Don't quarrel and raise your voice.

Jesus is our example for restraint while sharing our beliefs. One more reality should help us. Yes, there are opponents—hard-core opponents. But look more carefully. Some who hear our witness are bruised reeds or smoldering wicks. Like Jesus, we need to turn our attention to those who may need the message we share. They may be suffering and need the reminder of the gentle Shepherd's grace and mercy. Even the hard-core opponents can be turned from opposition. Jesus demonstrated Solomon's advice: "Gracious words are like a honeycomb, sweetness to the soul and health to the body" (Proverbs 16:24).

Even in those days of opposition for Jesus, large crowds sought him out. Their bruised and smoldering hearts yearned for his words of love, forgiveness, life, joy, and hope. Later, some of them may have become part of the host of believers who swarmed the earth with the gospel they had heard Jesus proclaim. Perhaps even some of the Pharisees became part of that swarm.

Harsh words do not soothe or make an argument stronger. They only harden opinions and attitudes. When we face opposition for our faith in Jesus and his Word, Jesus shows us a better strategy than raising our voices and responding with anger.

PRAYER: Jesus, how often I have fallen into the trap of an emotional or angry response when someone opposes me because I trust you. Help me set aside my initial reactions and speak with grace, love, and commitment. Help me bring your healing Word to the bruised reeds that surround me every day. Amen.

5

Forgiveness and Love

One of the Pharisees asked [Jesus] to eat with him, and he went into the Pharisee's house and reclined at table. And behold, a woman of the city, who was a sinner, when she learned that he was reclining at table in the Pharisee's house, brought an alabaster flask of ointment, and standing behind him at his feet, weeping, she began to wet his feet with her tears and wiped them with the hair of her head and kissed his feet and anointed them with the ointment. Now when the Pharisee who had invited him saw this, he said to himself, "If this man were a prophet, he would have known who and what sort of woman this is who is touching him, for she is a sinner." And Jesus answering said to him, "Simon, I have something to say to you." And he answered, "Say it, Teacher." "A certain moneylender had two debtors. One owed five hundred denarii, and the other fifty. When they could not pay, he cancelled the debt of both. Now which of them will love him more?" Simon answered, "The one, I suppose, for whom he cancelled the larger debt." And he said to him, "You have judged rightly." Then turning toward the woman he said to Simon, "Do you see this woman? I entered your house; you gave me no water for my feet, but she has wet my feet with her tears and wiped them with her hair. You gave me no kiss, but from the time I came in she has not ceased to kiss my feet. You did not anoint my head with oil, but she has anointed my feet with ointment. Therefore I tell you, her sins, which are many, are forgiven—for she loved much. But he who is forgiven little, loves little." And he said to her, "Your sins are forgiven." Then those who were at table with him began to say among themselves, "Who is this, who even forgives sins?" And he said to the woman, "Your faith has saved you; go in peace." (Luke 7:36-50)

Perhaps all of the Pharisees were interested in what Jesus was doing. His miracles and his words were the talk of Judea and Galilee.

Nicodemus had come to Jesus privately under the cover of night because he believed that Jesus' miracles proved he had come from God. Nicodemus had learned a great deal that night as he listened to Jesus.

Some Pharisees stood on the sidelines, not sure what to make of Jesus. Some took a more active role. This Pharisee invited Jesus into his house for dinner and included some of his friends, probably other Pharisees, to join him in entertaining this remarkable guest. Putting the best construction on the gathering, these spiritual leaders may have wanted to know more about Jesus and his message so they could speak clearly about him. We don't know what they expected to hear and learn from Jesus, but they did get a lesson—one intended for us too.

The lesson came from an uninvited guest—a woman with the kind of history everyone talked about. She had lived a sinful life, but something in her life had changed. She heard that Jesus was at the Pharisee's house and came, uninvited, to anoint Jesus with expensive perfume.

She didn't want to anoint Jesus quietly, without notice. She walked into the Pharisee's house and was noticed immediately. As the guests were reclining for the meal, she made her way to Jesus. She anointed his feet, kissed them, and wet them with her tears of remorse. Then she wiped his feet with her hair. Her presence caused a stir and, as if that wasn't enough, the sweet smell of the perfume interrupted conversation and turned heads, even those who wanted to avoid looking at her. All eyes were on her, the invited guests were shocked, and the room must have been suddenly silent.

Then the murmuring began. In judgment, the host said to himself, "If this man were a prophet, he would have known who and what sort of woman this is who is touching him." He revealed his disdain for and opposition to Jesus. How could Jesus be a prophet? Jesus chose this moment to help this Pharisee learn an important lesson: Forgiveness motivates one to love.

Jesus did this with a question and a pointed illustration. Who loves more, the one who is forgiven much or the one who is forgiven little? The woman understood her status with God. She had failed to live as the law required. She no doubt heard Jesus speak of forgiveness somewhere and understood what Isaiah wrote: "Though your sins are like scarlet, they shall be as white as snow" (Isaiah 1:18). She was cleansed and deeply grateful. Her gratitude moved her to show how deeply she appreciated the forgiveness Jesus promised.

Jesus also pointedly applied the lesson to the Pharisee. When Jesus entered his house, the Pharisee did not offer the common courtesies generally offered to guests—not even the customary water to wash dust from his sandaled feet or a kiss, which was a customary greeting. Jesus was there to be tested, observed, and evaluated. Love and appreciation for his grace and forgiveness were not part of the Pharisees' agenda.

Yet in the face of that attitude, Jesus challenged Simon the Pharisee to examine himself. Was he a sinner? Did he understand that all people are sinners before God, that not all may be guilty of a sinful life like the woman but all are still in need of forgiveness? Jesus was inviting Simon to recognize his sinfulness, his lack of love, and to embrace the forgiveness that was for him as well as all others.

Some failed to see their own sin and remained in their moral superiority and arrogance. Forgiveness? Perhaps some asked, "Why do I need forgiveness?" Instead of looking at their own sins, they attacked Jesus: "Who is this, who even forgives sins?" This continues to be a common tactic for those who oppose Jesus. Instead of admitting the unworthiness of all humans, they deflect the pointed accusation of sin and shift the focus away from them to another issue. Here the issue is the authority of Jesus. But Jesus continued to challenge them to consider their status before God when he turned to the woman and said, "Your faith has saved you; go in peace." She loved Jesus because she was forgiven.

PRAYER: Lord Jesus, I believe that I am altogether sinful from birth, but you have washed and cleansed me of my sin. I am grateful. I ask that you help me show my love for you in all I do. Help me willingly to bring you tokens of my love, not only in the way I live but also in my offerings. Create in me the spirit of this woman who knew your forgiveness and then showed how deeply she loved you. Amen.

6

Possessed by Beelzebul

Then [Jesus] went home, and the crowd gathered again, so that they could not even eat. And when his family heard it, they went out to seize him, for they were saying, "He is out of his mind." And the scribes who came down from Jerusalem were saying, "He is possessed by Beelzebul," and "by the prince of demons he casts out the demons." And he called them to him and said to them in parables, "How can Satan cast out Satan? If a kingdom is divided against itself, that kingdom cannot stand. And if a house is divided against itself, that house will not be able to stand. Truly, I say to you, all sins will be forgiven the children of man, and whatever blasphemies they utter, but whoever blasphemes against the Holy Spirit never has forgiveness, but is guilty of an eternal sin"—for they were saying, "He has an unclean spirit." And his mother and his brothers came, and standing outside they sent to him and called him. And a crowd was sitting around him, and they said to him, "Your mother and your brothers are outside, seeking you." And he answered them, "Who are my mother and my brothers?" And looking about at those who sat around him, he said, "Here are my mother and my brothers! For whoever does the will of God, he is my brother and sister and mother." (Mark 3:20-25,28-35)

When one tactic fails to reach your goal, another must take its place. The accusation that Jesus broke the Sabbath and encouraged his disciples to do the same had been laid to rest for two reasons. First, Jesus had spoken so clearly about mercy even on the Sabbath that the argument of the Pharisees could not stand. Second, Jesus asserted he had the power as Lord of the Sabbath to teach the Sabbath regulations because he was responsible for them in the first place. He asserted he was God.

So with that objection laid to rest, the enemies of Jesus chose another approach. They could not deny what he had been doing—his miracles and his preaching. The miracles were clearly like nothing they had ever seen before. Yet they would not believe that he was God come to earth. Their thinking required another explanation—another tactic to oppose him.

Even Jesus' family members had difficulty with his claim that he was the anointed, promised deliverer—the Christ. Their explanation was directed more toward his activities. He was so busy being surrounded by crowds craving his healing touch that he and his disciples didn't have time to eat. "They went out to seize him." The reason? "He [was] out of his mind." They thought he needed someone to protect him and look after him. A time of seclusion was their prescription. That would give him time to recover. To his family, Jesus may have appeared to be manic, hyper, or overexcited. So rest and quiet was their solution.

That is one way to view their efforts, but they may have had a darker motive. Were they offended by Jesus? Did the opposition of the Pharisees to Jesus also blacken their reputations? As members of Jesus' family, they were naturally associated in the minds of the crowds with this maniac man. We don't really know whether they were concerned for Jesus, sought to avoid some opposition themselves, or had another reason. All we know is that they took steps to bring calm to their agitated relative and perhaps to themselves too.

The goal of the Pharisees was to discredit Jesus. They said that he was "possessed" and drew his power from the prince of the demons—Beelzebul. Name-calling and attacking one's motivation is a classic way to discredit an opponent. We've all been in arguments with others. When they cannot overcome the points we make, they begin to attack us personally. Unfortunately, when that happens, we too often resort to the same tactic. We may even raise our voices and shout at our opponent, using derogatory names in our angry words. Sadly, we take the bait and the discussion escalates into a shouting match where no one listens to anyone.

Jesus took a different path. He remained calm. But more than that, he offered a clear reason why their criticism was impossible. He did not call them names or treat them with disdain. He asked a simple question:

"How can Satan cast out Satan?" Their criticism made no logical sense. He didn't say their thinking was stupid and illogical. He didn't call them fools. He simply pointed out that their thinking would lead to chaos not only in the world but also in Satan's kingdom. The proverb he gave was clear to everyone, no matter what they thought of Jesus: "If a kingdom is divided against itself, that kingdom cannot stand."

Jesus took one step more. He issued a warning to them about their opposition to him. Were they coming close to the sin against the Holy Spirit? Were they closing their minds and locking the doors to their hearts so that the Holy Spirit could not enter? Their attitude might grow to an unyielding rejection to the gracious words of Jesus—an obstinate, deliberate, and persistent refusal to listen to the gospel Jesus offered. That would prevent the Holy Spirit access to their hearts. It's like stopping your ears to prevent even an important word or idea from entering. Jesus was God's Anointed who was sent to "proclaim good news" (Isaiah 61:1-3). They were refusing to listen. Some would persist in rejecting Jesus to their dying day. Others, like the Pharisee Saul, even though he persecuted Christians, would come to believe in Jesus as God's Anointed, the Christ.

Then Jesus issued a gentle and gracious lesson. His mother and brothers wanted his attention. Perhaps they had finally come to take charge of him. When informed of their presence, he looked at those who were around him listening to his message with open hearts. Then, referring to those who were listening to him, he said, "Here are my mother and my brothers!" They were doing God's will, listening to him. They had not shut their hearts and coldly rejected him. Those who had come to listen were the opposite of the Pharisees who claimed Jesus was driven by the power of Satan.

PRAYER: Lord Jesus, keep my ears open to your gracious gospel so that the Holy Spirit may continue to nurture and strengthen my faith. When I am opposed because I trust in you, keep me from anger and personal attacks against those who oppose me. Fill my mind and heart with love for my enemies so that I may speak words of truth with gentleness and compassion. For your sake, Lord Jesus. Amen.

7

Need for a Sign

Then some of the scribes and Pharisees answered him, saying, "Teacher, we wish to see a sign from you." But he answered them, "An evil and adulterous generation seeks for a sign, but no sign will be given to it except the sign of the prophet Jonah. For just as Jonah was three days and three nights in the belly of the great fish, so will the Son of Man be three days and three nights in the heart of the earth. The men of Nineveh will rise up at the judgment with this generation and condemn it, for they repented at the preaching of Jonah, and behold, something greater than Jonah is here." (Matthew 12:38-41)

The request of the Pharisees and teachers seemed reasonable. "We wish to see a sign from you." Jesus' response could have been, "Haven't you been watching and listening?" The miracles of Jesus were in the memories and on the lips of thousands who had come to see and listen to Jesus. Jesus had healed a man with a shriveled hand in a synagogue on the Sabbath. The Pharisees had reacted to that miracle by plotting the death of Jesus. So there must have been something more behind this request.

There was! The Pharisees did not accept what Jesus said and what he taught. He claimed to be Lord of the Sabbath and chided them for their lack of understanding of Scripture's message about David, the priests, and mercy on the Sabbath. His answers to their questions about the Sabbath had been a not so gentle reminder to reconsider their opposition. Instead, his answers stung and embarrassed them. When he healed the man in the synagogue on the Sabbath, their hearts were not moved to repentance but hardened to anything Jesus said or did. Not only did they plot to kill him, but they also accused him of casting out demons by the power of Beelzebul.

Why come back to Jesus with this call for a sign? The proof they seemed to want was in the list of things Jesus had already done. They could have asked any one of those who had come to listen to him or seek his aid. But they knew what those people would say. Like Nicodemus, they would have said, "We know that you are a teacher come from God, for no one can do these signs that you do unless God is with him" (John 3:2). Nicodemus was one of them—a Pharisee. But his heart was not made of stony opposition. It was open to listen when Jesus said, "God so loved the world, that he gave his only Son, that whoever believes in him should not perish but have eternal life" (John 3:16).

We might assume there were other Pharisees whose hearts were not made of stone, but the leadership, like a wall, stood firmly against Jesus. "Show us a sign. Right now prove to us that you are more than a charlatan and speak with the authority of God." He already had. But they were not listening, and they would not have believed even if Jesus had performed a miracle. They wanted Jesus to conform to their agenda and follow their direction. "Do it now!"

PRAYER: Lord Jesus, send me your Holy Spirit through your Word always and especially when you speak to me in parables. Grant me understanding and insight so that I see correctly the messages you send me through parables like that of the sower and the seed. Prepare my heart and mind to be fertile soil for all of your Word so that I grow in understanding and faith. Amen.

8

The Parable of the Sower

That same day Jesus went out of the house and sat beside the sea. And great crowds gathered about him, so that he got into a boat and sat down. And the whole crowd stood on the beach. And he told them many things in parables, saying: "A sower went out to sow. And as he sowed, some seeds fell along the path, and the birds came and devoured them. Other seeds fell on rocky ground, where they did not have much soil, and immediately they sprang up, since they had no depth of soil, but when the sun rose they were scorched. And since they had no root, they withered away. Other seeds fell among thorns, and the thorns grew up and choked them. Other seeds fell on good soil and produced grain, some a hundredfold, some sixty, some thirty. He who has ears, let him hear." Then the disciples came and said to him, "Why do you speak to them in parables?" And he answered them, "To you it has been given to know the secrets of the kingdom of heaven, but to them it has not been given. For to the one who has, more will be given, and he will have an abundance, but from the one who has not, even what he has will be taken away. This is why I speak to them in parables, because seeing they do not see, and hearing they do not hear, nor do they understand. Hear then the parable of the sower: When anyone hears the word of the kingdom and does not understand it, the evil one comes and snatches away what has been sown in his heart. This is what was sown along the path. As for what was sown on rocky ground, this is the one who hears the word and immediately receives it with joy, yet he has no root in himself, but endures for a while, and when tribulation or persecution arises on account of the word, immediately he falls away. As for what was sown among thorns, this is the one who hears the word, but the cares of the world and the deceitfulness of riches choke the word, and it proves unfruitful. As for what was sown on good soil, this is the one who hears the word and understands it. He indeed bears fruit and yields, in one case a hundredfold, in another sixty, and in another thirty." (Matthew 13:1-13,18-23)

How often have we sat beside a lake and simply watched the waves play on the shore? For us, it's often a quiet time for relaxation and peace. For Jesus, such times of relaxation and peace came infrequently. He had to steal away to a quiet place to pray, and he encouraged his disciples to come with him (Mark 6:31). But this was not one of those times for quiet reflection at the lakeside. Jesus and his disciples were surrounded by a large crowd.

Jesus got into a boat. Perhaps it was one owned and operated by the fishing business of Peter, Andrew, James, and John. Earlier he had used a boat to help his disciples escape the crowd while he went to a mountainside to pray (Mark 6:46). But not this time. The boat gave him an excellent setting for teaching while the crowd stood along the shore. No doubt the crowd included some who were deeply committed to Jesus and eagerly consumed his every word. But there is also no doubt it also included some who were not committed and opposed him and his teaching.

Jesus taught in parables. Matthew, Mark, and Luke relate the parable of the sower in a series of parables. We aren't sure exactly when these parables were taught in the ministry of Jesus. The writers of the gospels are less concerned with accurate chronology than they are with the events and their meaning.

Like most parables, this parable is a simple, everyday event Jesus used to teach the crowd about spiritual and eternal truths. The parables were a means to help people remember the truths he taught. We learn difficult concepts better by hearing a story than by hearing a lecture. We also remember the lesson more clearly for a longer time. That would be important to the faithful who were there—including his 12 disciples. After Jesus ascended, when they would be responsible for teaching others what Jesus had said, these parables would bring to mind the truths Jesus had taught them. It is often easier for us to read and remember the gospel accounts of Jesus—the stories—than to read and remember the lessons in the epistles. That's especially true for new Christians.

Jesus ended the parable by saying, "He who has ears, let him hear." Was he hiding something? The disciples came to Jesus afterward. They wondered why he taught in parables. He said, "To you it has been given to know the secrets of the kingdom of heaven, but to them it has not been given." That seems like a curious response, but the crowd that day included both disciples and enemies. Those opposed to Jesus had already revealed their strategy. They were looking for an opportunity to attack him and had accused him of doing miracles by the power of the devil. No matter what he said, they would not believe but instead tried to find a way to attack him. They had no ears to hear! Instead, they bent everything Jesus said and fashioned his words into an attack.

Jesus used parables not only to teach those who had ears to hear but also to hide the truth from his enemies and frustrate their efforts to confuse others and speak against him. The parable was a simple story. The Pharisees probably asked the same question as the disciples: "Why do you speak to them in parables?" The hearts and ears of Jesus' enemies were calloused, closed, and hard. They didn't get the message, but the believers did. Their efforts to destroy Jesus were disarmed and frustrated by parables like the sower and the seed.

The disciples were also a bit confused at first about the meaning of the parable. They came to Jesus to ask for his explanation. That too was an important reason to teach the parables. Ask Jesus! He knows! And they did. Those whose hearts and ears were closed would not come to Jesus. Those who trusted him for the truth would come. Their hearts and ears were open and willing to be taught. They knew he loved them even if they did not understand everything.

The explanation Jesus gave them is a beautiful story of how the gospel works when it is shared with others. Some will simply let it lie without any concerns. Some will listen but have too many other concerns. Others will hear but let the message wither. Finally, some will listen, believe, and grow in various ways.

What a lesson for the disciples and for us. The kingdom of heaven is about sowing the seed of the gospel. These disciples would eventually be sent out to make disciples of all nations by teaching the gospel. Their work would not be successful in bringing all to faith, but it would bring some. Sowing seed was and is the work of the kingdom. Jesus' words apply to us as they did long ago: "Go . . . make disciples of all nations, . . . teaching them . . . all that I have commanded you" (Matthew 28:19-20).

PRAYER: Lord Jesus, keep my ears open to your words. When I am confused or troubled by your words, warm my heart with the promise of your love so that my heart will not be hardened to your truth. Draw me back to your words in the Scriptures so that I may be filled with your truth and eager to share it. Always give me eager ears to hear. Amen.

9

More Parables

[Jesus] put another parable before them, saying, "The kingdom of heaven may be compared to a man who sowed good seed in his field, but while his men were sleeping, his enemy came and sowed weeds among the wheat and went away. So when the plants came up and bore grain, then the weeds appeared also. And the servants of the master of the house came and said to him, 'Master, did you not sow good seed in your field? How then does it have weeds?' He said to them, 'An enemy has done this.' So the servants said to him, 'Then do you want us to go and gather them?' But he said, 'No, lest in gathering the weeds you root up the wheat along with them. Let both grow together until the harvest, and at harvest time I will tell the reapers, "Gather the weeds first and bind them in bundles to be burned, but gather the wheat into my barn."'" He put another parable before them, saying, "The kingdom of heaven is like a grain of mustard seed that a man took and sowed in his field. It is the smallest of all seeds, but when it has grown it is larger than all the garden plants and becomes a tree, so that the birds of the air come and make nests in its branches." He told them another parable. "The kingdom of heaven is like leaven that a woman took and hid in three measures of flour, till it was all leavened." All these things Jesus said to the crowds in parables; indeed, he said nothing to them without a parable. This was to fulfill what was spoken by the prophet: "I will open my mouth in parables; I will utter what has been hidden since the foundation of the world." (Matthew 13:24-35)

In the parable of the sower, Jesus identified the seed as the "word of God" (Luke 8:11) and the "word of the kingdom" (Matthew 13:19). Both Mark and Luke tell us that Jesus told the Twelve and others the meaning of the parable when he was alone with them. Matthew includes it immediately after the telling of the parable. The key feature of the parable is the reaction to the Word of God, the gospel.

Jesus had more to say about the gospel and the reaction to it. Perhaps he included these parables there at the lakeside. That is a reasonable assertion since the next parable is also about sowing seed. Or these parables may have been taught on another occasion and Matthew lumped them together because they are related. Remembering these parables together after Jesus ascended would be a natural grouping because they are all related to "the seed."

The disciples were given the command to teach all nations when Jesus had finished his work. They were the sowers. What a wonderful reminder to them and to us as well that the reaction to the gospel will not be the same for every person. Some will not listen. Some will eagerly receive it, but their faith will dry up and wither in the face of trials and persecution. Others will be distracted by the things of this world and forget about the kingdom of God and its blessings. And still others will persevere through troubles and temptations to be fruitful believers in the kingdom of God. Disciples of Jesus in every age have seen these reactions to the gospel.

Jesus told his disciples of one more reaction. The seed that fell on the good ground with the blessing of the Holy Spirit produced believers. That is now our focus. What happens to those who become disciples of Jesus in the world? They live with those who are not disciples—the weeds of the parable. Perhaps this parable was easier than other parables for the disciples to understand. They were with Jesus and identified with him, but they knew that not everyone they met was a disciple. The Pharisees kept assailing Jesus. Those who do not believe would also assail believers throughout history. It was an important reminder for the disciples, and it is a reminder for us too.

Jesus told another parable. This one was a reminder of the blessings believers have in the kingdom of God. The seed again appears, but this time as a mustard seed. Jesus chose a mustard seed because it is "the smallest of all seeds." If we identify it as the gospel, the choice fits. The gospel is not the earthquake or the fire but the gentle whisper of God's love for sinners (1 Kings 19:11-13). Discounted by so many, nevertheless, it is "the power of God for salvation" (Romans 1:16). It works to produce believers who become like "a tree planted by streams of water" (Psalm 1:3; see also Isaiah 44:1-5 and Isaiah 61:1-3: "oaks of righteousness"). As believers grow and mature, they become a place of refuge. The kingdom of God is the result of the planting of the gospel, and it becomes larger as these believers share the gospel with others.

As a reminder of the influence that believers have in this world, Jesus told still another parable. The kingdom of heaven is like yeast. The believers in this world—the yeast—always seem small and insignificant compared to the rest of humanity—the flour. But they produce the fruit of the Spirit, as Paul describes in Galatians: "love, joy, peace, patience, kindness, goodness, faithfulness, gentleness, self-control" (Galatians 5:22-23). These blessings have value and importance not only for believers but also for all of humanity. Believers are salt, as Jesus said in his Sermon on the Mount. Another way to look at the parable is that the yeast works within believers' hearts and influences every part of their lives. Either way, Jesus was underscoring the importance of being a believer in this world.

Matthew lists one more reason Jesus taught in parables. He was teaching things "hidden since the foundation of the world." These truths were new and fresh proclamations of God's truth. They were New Testament teachings built on Moses, the psalms, and the prophets. They were bright gems hidden in the pages of prophecy of the Savior's coming. Jesus was polishing them for all to see. What a treasure the disciples had in these parables as they went out into the world to sow the gospel. What a treasure we have as well.

We live in a world where we rub shoulders with unbelievers at every turn. We should not despair or seek to be like the world. Jesus reminds us of the fate of unbelievers. He also reminds us that while the church, the gospel, and believers—the kingdom of God—are discounted as small and insignificant, the kingdom is made up of trees of righteousness, a refuge for the weary who seek answers and comfort in the face of everyday life. By the power of the Holy Spirit, we influence others around us. That is why God puts us here in this world wherever we may be.

PRAYER: Lord Jesus, you have planted me here in this place for this time. Help me live as your disciple and seize every opportunity to do good to others and love others. Help me provide shelter to those who are weary, weak, or wandering. May they hear from my lips the sweet comfort of your Word. Then work in their hearts so they may also treasure your promises. For the sake of your kingdom. Amen.

10

The Kingdom of Heaven Is Like . . .

Then [Jesus] left the crowds and went into the house. And his disciples came to him, saying, "Explain to us the parable of the weeds of the field." He answered, "The one who sows the good seed is the Son of Man. The field is the world, and the good seed is the sons of the kingdom. The weeds are the sons of the evil one, and the enemy who sowed them is the devil. The harvest is the end of the age, and the reapers are angels. Just as the weeds are gathered and burned with fire, so will it be at the end of the age. The Son of Man will send his angels, and they will gather out of his kingdom all causes of sin and all law-breakers, and throw them into the fiery furnace. In that place there will be weeping and gnashing of teeth. Then the righteous will shine like the sun in the kingdom of their Father. He who has ears, let him hear. The kingdom of heaven is like treasure hidden in a field, which a man found and covered up. Then in his joy he goes and sells all that he has and buys that field. Again, the kingdom of heaven is like a merchant in search of fine pearls, who, on finding one pearl of great value, went and sold all that he had and bought it. Again, the kingdom of heaven is like a net that was thrown into the sea and gathered fish of every kind. When it was full, men drew it ashore and sat down and sorted the good into containers but threw away the bad. So it will be at the end of the age. The angels will come out and separate the evil from the righteous and throw them into the fiery furnace. In that place there will be weeping and gnashing of teeth. Have you understood all these things?" They said to him, "Yes." (Matthew 13:36-51)

The series of parables Jesus was teaching explains so much. He introduced the parable of the weeds with the words "The kingdom of heaven is like . . ." He told two more parables with the same introduction. He was explaining the kingdom of heaven for his disciples and also confounding the concept of the kingdom of heaven for the Pharisees. The disciples seem to have understood the parables of the mustard seed and the yeast. But they did not yet have the depth of understanding to understand the parable of the weeds.

Jesus "left the crowds and went into the house." Who's house? Peter was a fisherman and may have lived in Capernaum. His house was only a few blocks from the synagogue and a short walk from the northern shore of the Sea of Galilee. The ruins of Peter's home, or one like it, are still visible in Capernaum. Jesus retreated there with his disciples.

Once the disciples reached the relative privacy of the house, they asked a question that had been burning inside them on the short walk. Alone with Jesus and away from the crowd, they asked, "Explain to us the parable of the weeds of the field." Their ears were open to the teaching of Jesus, but they did not understand fully. The principle is simple: "Ask, and it will be given to you" (Matthew 7:7). Jesus had said that in his Sermon on the Mount. So with their limitations, weaknesses, and uncertainties, the disciples came to Jesus. He wanted them to do that. He wants us to do that. Come to him. Go to his Word. Listen. Read. Then you will grow and understand.

The disciples' question opened the door for Jesus to give them important lessons about the kingdom of God. This series of parables taught them what they would see and experience during the days when Jesus was still with them. The parables also provided lessons for them for the days after he ascended and turned over the work of the kingdom to them.

Jesus explained that the kingdom of heaven is like a man sowing seed in a field. But the field was sabotaged by an enemy who sowed weeds in the field. As Jesus explained this parable, perhaps they remembered the parable of the sower. But this parable adds a sinister twist. Yes, the Son of Man sowed good seed. The disciples were a result of that sowing; they believed and desired to follow him. But Jesus and the disciples lived in a world that also contained people who did not believe. So it would always be. The kingdom of heaven exists in the real world with real people who have different ideas about Jesus.

Today, believers are not to rip out the unbelievers to purify the world. Instead, they are to wait for the Lord to judge the unbelievers. Believers are to grow and mature beside the unbelievers in this world. Such is the kingdom.

When Jesus ascended and sent the disciples out into the world, this parable provided important lessons. They would experience opposition as Jesus did. Some would be arrested by the Pharisees in Jerusalem. Stephen would be killed. But the believers were to grow and mature in that environment. The church grew. When the apostles and other believers left Jerusalem and carried the message of Jesus to all of the world, opposition arose. Some of them would be arrested and killed in other parts of the Roman world. But the believers were to grow where the Lord had planted them and let him take care of judgment. The lesson stretches to our age too. We live side by side with those who do not believe and some who oppose us for our faith in Jesus. The clarity of this lesson and its application to all ages is amazing.

Jesus provided two more parables intended to encourage his disciples. When the world opposed them and sought to silence them, they were to remember the great treasure they had. Jesus promised forgiveness and eternal life. Those treasures could not be found in any place but in Jesus. Those treasures are priceless, and believers should be willing to lose everything rather than give them up. These believers listened. Later, when faced with opposition that would even result in their torture, imprisonment, and death, they would cling to Jesus. Like Paul, they could say, "For to me to live is Christ, and to die is gain" (Philippians 1:21). Now the disciples said they understood.

PRAYER: Lord, you have made me a part of your kingdom and are my priceless treasure. When day-to-day trials come, help me focus on the blessings only you can provide. When I am ridiculed for my faith, focus my attention on those blessings so that I may not abandon treasures you have given me. When my eyes close in death, hold your cross before my eyes so that I may die in peace. For your sake. Amen.

11

Bread to Eat

[Jesus] withdrew from there in a boat to a desolate place by himself. But when the crowds heard it, they followed him on foot from the towns. When he went ashore he saw a great crowd, and he had compassion on them and healed their sick. Now when it was evening, the disciples came to him and said, "This is a desolate place, and the day is now over; send the crowds away to go into the villages and buy food for themselves." But Jesus said, "They need not go away; you give them something to eat." They said to him, "We have only five loaves here and two fish." And he said, "Bring them here to me." Then he ordered the crowds to sit down on the grass, and taking the five loaves and the two fish, he looked up to heaven and said a blessing. Then he broke the loaves and gave them to the disciples, and the disciples gave them to the crowds. And they all ate and were satisfied. And they took up twelve baskets full of the broken pieces left over. And those who ate were about five thousand men, besides women and children. (Matthew 14:13-21)

After Jesus explained the parables to his disciples, it is not clear what happened next. Matthew seems to take a topical approach to the ministry of Jesus. Mark and Luke are not consistently chronological. John wrote later than the others, filling in some of the gaps and giving us more of the sayings and dialogues of Jesus. We are following a general chronology for our study of Jesus during the year of opposition, but not an exact chronology. We are looking both topically and chronologically to concentrate on how Jesus responded to those who opposed him.

Matthew tells us that "when Jesus had finished these parables, he went away from there" (13:53), apparently from "the house" (13:1,36), probably in Capernaum. We assume that after the sower parable, Jesus continued to travel around the northern shore of the Sea of Galilee, perhaps visiting various synagogues on the Sabbaths.

Matthew tells us that Jesus went to the synagogue in Nazareth and was rejected. Luke records the rejection at Nazareth earlier (4:14-30) and in greater detail. Was this a second visit to Nazareth? Early or late, the first visit or the second, we are told of the opposition to Jesus. His hometown wondered who made him such a celebrity. His family members—his mother, Mary; brothers (James, Joseph, Simon, and Judas); and sisters—were part of the community. The residents of Nazareth took offense and wondered, "Where did this man get these things?" (Mark 6:2).

It is easy to see why Matthew inserted this account here after the parables of the seed and the treasure. His choice to insert it here seems to confirm that this incident was not a second visit to the synagogue in Nazareth but the same one. Matthew wanted to illustrate the practical realities of the parables he had just recorded. The reaction at Nazareth was a lesson in the kingdom of God. The sower was spreading the seed, but not all of it fell on good soil. Sometimes weeds grew up with the wheat. And not everyone treasured the blessings Jesus offered. The disciples did, but Nazareth harbored those who did not (Matthew 13:58).

Jesus does not engage their unbelief but moves on. Luke tells us that Jesus sent out his disciples to proclaim the kingdom of God and heal the sick (Luke 9:2). At this point, Matthew, Mark, and Luke tell us about Herod's explanation for the miracles that had recently been performed. Herod said, "This is John the Baptist. He has been raised from the dead; that is why these miraculous powers are at work in him" (Matthew 14:2). There is a backstory to Herod's comment. Herod had imprisoned John and later had him beheaded because of a foolish vow he made. If the seed of the Word had found the soil of Herod's heart, it did not take root but had been snatched by Satan. He looked no further for an explanation of the miracles of Jesus and his disciples.

The disciples finished their work and returned to Jesus. They gathered and reported to him all they had done (Mark 6:30). Jesus withdrew to a "desolate place." The withdrawal was by boat, but the solitary place soon turned into a noisy spot on the shore. The crowds, perhaps swelled because of the mission of the disciples, ran on foot from all the towns and got there before Jesus and his disciples. When Jesus arrived, a large crowd was waiting for him.

What happened next was important for the disciples, the crowd, and us. Jesus had compassion on the crowd. He had compassion for those people on the shore and viewed them as "sheep without a shepherd" (Mark 6:34). The Son of Man began to sow seed. He taught them. He would not turn them away without the message his Father sent him to proclaim. The crowd received the Word of Life, and the disciples had another lesson in what the kingdom was about—sowing the seed of the Word of God. We understand that lesson too, as well as the reason behind it: the Lord's compassion for helpless sheep. He loves us all and wants us all to understand the reason he came, even when the clouds of opposition mar the horizon.

Jesus taught one more lesson. He fed the crowd. First he had a lesson for the disciples and challenged them to feed the crowd, but they were helpless in the face of this huge crowd and incapable of providing food. Jesus provided the answer to their helpless and feeble response: "He ordered the crowds to sit down on the grass." With the meager resources the disciples found, Jesus fed five thousand men "besides women and children." The disciples had 12 basketfuls more than the crowd could eat. Here's the lesson: Jesus has the concern and power to take care of our human needs as well as our spiritual needs. His compassion for human beings like us is a gracious blessing we do not deserve. Like the crowd, we are often sheep without a shepherd, but Jesus teaches us that we have a caring and powerful Shepherd.

PRAYER: Jesus, help me see that your kingdom is all about sowing the seed of your Word and trusting in your power to create faith through it. When I see the weeds that also sprout or refuse to believe, draw me to you and your Word so that I may grow as your disciple and sow the seed when I have the opportunity. In my daily life, Lord, help me realize that you give me daily bread and all I need. Keep me thankful for every gracious blessing. Amen.

12

The Kingdom of Heaven

When the people saw the sign that he had done, they said, "This is indeed the Prophet who is to come into the world!" Perceiving then that they were about to come and take him by force to make him king, Jesus withdrew again to the mountain by himself. (John 6:14-15)

The feeding of this large crowd of five thousand men plus women and children had an effect on all who were there. All the gospel writers record it. John puts the miracle near the Jewish Passover (John 6:4)—one year, we assume, before Jesus entered Jerusalem to the shouts of "Hosanna! Blessed is he who comes in the name of the Lord" (John 12:13) and one year away from his crucifixion when Pilate placed a placard on his cross that read, "Jesus of Nazareth, the King of the Jews" (John 19:19).

The miracle brings to mind two Old Testament miracles. The first is the way God fed his people with manna in the wilderness. No doubt, the people who had filled their stomachs with this bread and fish lunch recalled that miracle too. The second miracle is Elijah and the widow of Zarephath. The widow's handful of flour and a little oil were replenished again and again to keep her, her son, and Elijah alive (1 Kings 17).

Those in the crowd began to entertain the fulfillment of a long-held hope. "This is indeed the Prophet who is to come into the world!" That hope was for a future deliverer foretold so long ago. The Scriptures said he would be like Moses (Deuteronomy 18:15). Didn't the feeding of this crowd echo the manna in the wilderness when Moses led their ancestors? Who could argue the point? The prophecies also identified him as a great victorious warrior. Isaiah had written that this victor would proclaim, "I trampled down the peoples in my anger; I made them drunk in my wrath, and I poured out their lifeblood on the earth"

(Isaiah 63:6). Could Jesus be the one to restore the nation's grandeur and defeat its enemies, including the Roman legions?

The people had longed for such a deliverer and thought they needed to seize the opportunity and start the new age for their nation. The disciples of Jesus did not rush to join in this grassroots enthusiasm. Jesus had schooled them in what the kingdom of heaven is: planting the seed of the gospel. It is finding treasure in God's love for flawed and sinful creatures. It is growing to produce fruits of faith as Jesus had told them in his parables.

Overthrowing the oppressive powers of the nation was not part of the message of Jesus. Yes, the disciples had witnessed his power to heal and even still storms, but they listened to his words announcing forgiveness, life, and hope and heard no revolutionary rhetoric—no slogans that could be used to drum up support or motivate political change. Somewhere, there was one rebel who would stoke the flames of insurrection—Barabbas (Mark 15:7). He would be arrested and appear in Jerusalem at the time of the next Passover. But the disciples knew a different Jesus who would "not cry aloud or lift up his voice, or make it heard in the street" (Isaiah 42:2).

The disciples did not yet grasp the full implications of the differences between Barabbas and Jesus, but they knew Jesus was no rebel. The people in the crowd were convinced that Jesus would lead them to freedom and victory over the Romans. Attempting to correct them at this point would have proved futile and only encouraged their misunderstanding. Jesus understood what they wanted. He withdrew to a mountain to be by himself.

The disciples were left with the crowd still there on the grass. As the day wore on and the evening approached, they too decided to leave the crowd. In the growing darkness, they boarded a boat and headed toward Capernaum.

It appeared that the miracle was over, but the crowd didn't simply disappear and go to their homes. Some stayed, perhaps discussing the events of the day and entertaining the possibility that Jesus might eventually lead them to freedom and glory. So the discussion about the bread and Jesus would continue. John gives us the details of that discussion the day after.

We know what opposition to Jesus looks like most of the time. The Jewish leaders gave us a good look at open hostility and opposition. But those who wanted to make Jesus a king were a different sort. They didn't want what Jesus had to offer—the kingdom of heaven. Instead, their expectations were not heaven bound. They were what they wanted and needed here in this life—like bread, political freedom, victory over enemies, and removal of oppression. Those are excellent goals for us here in this life, but Jesus would challenge these people to see a different horizon.

All too often, we want to make Jesus the supplier of our needs, like a quartermaster or fulfillment center we can use to order food, clothing, shelter, freedom, happiness, family, joy, and hope for the future. But it's time to listen to Jesus tell us what he came to give us. John's account of the feeding of the five thousand shares with us how Jesus tried to lift the vision of these people from bread to heaven.

PRAYER: Lord Jesus, I am grateful for all the blessings you provide—food, clothing, shelter, financial resources, and all I need for my body and life. As I make use of all your blessings, help me see beyond them all to the greater blessings. You won those blessings for me by shedding your blood. You sacrificed your body and life for me. May I never lose sight of those blessings in my concern for my body and welfare. Keep my eyes on the real treasures. Amen.

13

Bread of Life

Other boats from Tiberias came near the place where they had eaten the bread after the Lord had given thanks. So when the crowd saw that Jesus was not there, nor his disciples, they themselves got into the boats and went to Capernaum, seeking Jesus. When they found him on the other side of the sea, they said to him, "Rabbi, when did you come here?" Jesus answered them, "Truly, truly, I say to you, you are seeking me, not because you saw signs, but because you ate your fill of the loaves. Do not work for the food that perishes, but for the food that endures to eternal life, which the Son of Man will give to you. For on him God the Father has set his seal." Then they said to him, "What must we do, to be doing the works of God?" Jesus answered them, "This is the work of God, that you believe in him whom he has sent." So they said to him, "Then what sign do you do, that we may see and believe you? What work do you perform? Our fathers ate the manna in the wilderness; as it is written, 'He gave them bread from heaven to eat.'" Jesus then said to them, "Truly, truly, I say to you, it was not Moses who gave you the bread from heaven, but my Father gives you the true bread from heaven. For the bread of God is he who comes down from heaven and gives life to the world." They said to him, "Sir, give us this bread always." Jesus said to them, "I am the bread of life; whoever comes to me shall not hunger, and whoever believes in me shall never thirst. But I said to you that you have seen me and yet do not believe. All that the Father gives me will come to me, and whoever comes to me I will never cast out. For I have come down from heaven, not to do my own will but the will of him who sent me. And this is the will of him who sent me, that I should lose nothing of all that he has given me, but raise it up on the last day. For this is the will of my Father, that everyone who looks on the Son and believes in him should have eternal life, and I will raise him up on the last day." So the Jews grumbled about him, because he said, "I am the bread that came down from heaven." They said, "Is not this Jesus, the son of Joseph, whose father and mother we know? How does he now say, 'I have come down from heaven'?" (John 6:23-42)

The night after the feeding of the five thousand was a night to remember for the disciples. Jesus had directed his disciples to go on ahead of him while he dismissed the crowd. Then he went up to a mountainside to be by himself and to pray. In the meantime, the disciples were having a difficult time against the wind and waves. As they rowed against the wind, Jesus came to them, walking on the water. He identified himself and told them not to be afraid. Peter suggested, "Lord, if it is you, command me to come to you on the water" (Matthew 14:28). Jesus invited Peter to come, and Peter stepped over the side of the boat and walked toward Jesus. But he soon grew frightened and sank, crying, "Lord, save me." Jesus reached for Peter, and soon Peter and the others were safely at their destination (Matthew 14:22-33).

The crowd reappeared in Capernaum. When the people recognized Jesus, word spread through the surrounding countryside. Some came wondering how Jesus had gotten from the grassy plain where he had fed them. Jesus challenged them to look deeper than the bread they had received. "Do not work for the food that perishes, but for the food that endures to eternal life, which the Son of Man will give to you."

They recognized that Jesus was taking the conversation to a deeper spiritual meaning and asked, "What must we do, to be doing the works of God?" They wanted that eternal life from the Son of Man, and they wanted to know what to do in order to receive it. They were not thinking of the undeserved gift of God's grace but wondering how to earn eternal life by their efforts—a standard notion of the human mind. Jesus' answer pointed them instead toward grace: "This is the work of God, that you believe in him whom he has sent."

The one whom God had sent was there right before them. He had given them food the day before and had suddenly appeared in Capernaum in a way they did not understand. The disciples had also witnessed another miracle on the stormy sea that confirmed Jesus as the one sent by God. The people wanted a sign. But Jesus had already given several signs.

Jesus challenged them to look beyond Moses. The source of the manna was not Moses. It was "my Father," Jesus said. More important than the manna or the bread they had eaten the day before was the true bread that comes down from heaven and gives life to the world. Expand your thinking, Jesus challenged. They understood his encouragement on one level but had not yet broken through the limitations of human thought about food: "Sir, give us this bread always."

"I am the bread of life." In those words, Jesus was asserting that he had come down from above. He is greater than Moses, who in their minds had given their ancestors bread to sustain life in the wilderness. That bread spoiled, as Jesus had said. Jesus invited them to see him as the provider of eternal life. "This is the will of my Father, that everyone who looks on the Son and believes in him should have eternal life." That's what he had come down from heaven to give to all believers.

The people stumbled. Jesus was claiming he was the one who came from heaven. There he was before them as plain as day. They had seen him provide bread that filled their bellies. Jesus said, "You have seen me and yet do not believe." They grumbled about what Jesus had said. They did not accept his claim that he had come down from heaven. What they saw was the flesh and blood human called Jesus. How could he be more? How could a mere human promise eternal life? Jesus would not yet abandon them in their questions and doubts. On this day he continued to challenge them to see him as true God and true man come to earth to provide eternal life.

PRAYER: Lord Jesus, you give me daily bread to sustain my life. Stretch my thinking so I might see that your blessings are far beyond this life. In good days and bad, keep me focused on the blessings of eternal life that are waiting for me. May my faith be like that of Job: "I know that my Redeemer lives, and at the last he will stand upon the earth. And after my skin has been thus destroyed, yet in my flesh I shall see God, whom I shall see for myself, and my eyes shall behold, and not another" (Job 19:25-27). Amen.

14

Hard Sayings

Jesus answered them, "Do not grumble among yourselves. No one can come to me unless the Father who sent me draws him. And I will raise him up on the last day. It is written in the Prophets, 'And they will all be taught by God.' Everyone who has heard and learned from the Father comes to me—not that anyone has seen the Father except he who is from God; he has seen the Father. Truly, truly, I say to you, whoever believes has eternal life. I am the bread of life. Your fathers ate the manna in the wilderness, and they died. This is the bread that comes down from heaven, so that one may eat of it and not die. I am the living bread that came down from heaven. If anyone eats of this bread, he will live forever. And the bread that I will give for the life of the world is my flesh." The Jews then disputed among themselves, saying, "How can this man give us his flesh to eat?" So Jesus said to them, "Truly, truly, I say to you, unless you eat the flesh of the Son of Man and drink his blood, you have no life in you. Whoever feeds on my flesh and drinks my blood has eternal life, and I will raise him up on the last day. For my flesh is true food, and my blood is true drink. Whoever feeds on my flesh and drinks my blood abides in me, and I in him. As the living Father sent me, and I live because of the Father, so whoever feeds on me, he also will live because of me. This is the bread that came down from heaven, not like the bread the fathers ate, and died. Whoever feeds on this bread will live forever." Jesus said these things in the synagogue, as he taught at Capernaum. (John 6:43-59)

This dialogue with those who had eaten the bread Jesus provided was a discussion of eternal life and its source. Jesus said that those who had come to find him in Capernaum were looking for the wrong thing.

They were looking for someone who could give them bread to keep them alive until the next day, perhaps like Moses kept the people alive for 40 years in the wilderness. But Jesus said they should be looking for the bread from heaven—the true bread that gives eternal life to the world. Life! That is what they wanted. "Give us this bread always" (John 6:34).

But they were still thinking of bread like the manna God gave to his people in the wilderness or the bread from the loaves the day before. Jesus took the discussion a step further when he said, "I am the bread of life." This was no longer a discussion of where to get the best bread to eat with your family. It wasn't even about eating bread. Jesus said, "Everyone who looks on the Son and believes in him should have eternal life" (John 6:40).

This Bread of Life is the source of eternal life, and Jesus said clearly, "I am the bread of life." He identified what this discussion was really about. "This is the bread that comes down from heaven, so that one may eat of it and not die. I am the living bread that came down from heaven." We understand those clear words because we have faith in Jesus, the Bread of Life. They did not. What Jesus said was nonsense to them. How could he be the one come down from heaven? They knew his family members. He was like them. Objections like those of his family's neighbors in Nazareth appeared again. Then they understood that Jesus was making a bold claim about himself—even an arrogant claim in their minds.

Yet Jesus had also said clearly that his Father's will was to give eternal life to all who believed in the Son. So Jesus continued to challenge their understanding so they would abandon their unbelief and understand that he was the Savior who had come to earth to save the world. Remarkably, Jesus included a reference to events that would happen in Jerusalem a year later: "The bread that I will give for the life of the world is my flesh." We get it. They did not. Perhaps they would when they learned of his suffering and death.

Jesus does not abandon the discussion, nor does he throw his hands in the air in frustration with their inability to grasp what he was saying. He was saying the same thing he told Nicodemus: "God so loved the world, that he gave his only Son, that whoever believes in him should not perish but have eternal life" (John 3:16). So simple, but as simple as it was, it still created opposition and rejection.

We can learn from Jesus here. He continues to sow the seed of the Word. That Word may fall on the hard ground of human hearts unwilling to accept the gracious promises of eternal life. In some cases, the seed will be snatched away by Satan. The problem is not in the seed, which is life-giving, or with the Lord. It is within human hearts that resist the gospel. We are all enemies of God by nature, and our default reaction is to reject whatever God says. Like those in Capernaum, our sinful nature finds an excuse to refuse the message. "Is not this Jesus, the son of Joseph, whose father and mother we know? How does he now say, 'I have come down from heaven'?" (John 6:42).

We might not have the skill to engage people the way Jesus did here. Our efforts to tell others of the blessings Jesus gives will pale by comparison. But the people rejected the eloquence of Jesus. We should expect that people might also reject our efforts. Nevertheless, Jesus kept proclaiming the gospel. Perhaps some of the people listening to Jesus would believe later and Satan would miss his opportunity to snatch the seed from their hearts. It might lie dormant until a later time. So our goal should be to share the gospel as clearly as we know how and depend on the power of the Word to create faith and life.

PRAYER: Lord Jesus, I am sometimes frustrated when people think I believe in silly hopes and dreams. When I see all that they face—the trials of life, the heartaches, and even death itself—I do not understand how anyone could walk away from your promises. Yet, Lord, I ask that you give me the courage to speak your truth even when they reject it and me. When my words are awkward and seem to miss the mark, still send your Holy Spirit to work in their hearts. Help me always to depend on the power of the gospel. Amen.

15

Words of Life

When many of his disciples heard it, they said, "This is a hard saying; who can listen to it?" But Jesus, knowing in himself that his disciples were grumbling about this, said to them, "Do you take offense at this? Then what if you were to see the Son of Man ascending to where he was before? It is the Spirit who gives life; the flesh is no help at all. The words that I have spoken to you are spirit and life. But there are some of you who do not believe." (For Jesus knew from the beginning who those were who did not believe, and who it was who would betray him.) And he said, "This is why I told you that no one can come to me unless it is granted him by the Father." After this many of his disciples turned back and no longer walked with him. So Jesus said to the twelve, "Do you want to go away as well?" Simon Peter answered him, "Lord, to whom shall we go? You have the words of eternal life, and we have believed, and have come to know, that you are the Holy One of God." (John 6:60-69)

The words Jesus spoke were full of the Spirit and life. Those words were the gospel. In this exchange with those who had come to find him in the synagogue of Capernaum, Jesus did not argue as much as he sought to be clear. He was probing the limits of their thinking. They were talking of the bread that spoils; he was talking about the bread that gives eternal life. They were thinking of a magic baker who would give them bread to eat forever; he was helping them understand that he was no mere baker but God himself who had come down from heaven and had the power and authority to give eternal life.

"Many of his disciples" could not understand what he was saying. To them it was a hard saying. It was beyond their experience. It was heavenly wisdom, not earthly, practical knowledge, even if it was a simple message: "Truly, truly, I say to you, whoever believes has eternal life" (John 6:47).

Yes, the words he spoke were "the power of God for salvation to everyone" (Romans 1:16), as Paul would remind the Romans. But they refused it even if they understood it. Perhaps this was a failure to some. The faithful Twelve must have looked with anguished eyes at what happened as "many of his disciples turned back and no longer walked with him." The gospel message was foolishness to them. For the disciples it was different. The seed had sprouted within them, and they believed. Jesus had confirmed their faith in the answers to the questions they raised about the parables. In the miracle of the feeding of the five thousand and in his appearance to them in the storm the night before (John 6:16-21), they knew he had come from above.

Jesus turned to them. It was their turn to decide: Disappear with the rest or remain. The Spirit had worked in their hearts through the words Jesus had been sharing with them and the crowds. Some in the crowd believed. Some did not. Why some and not others? That's a question on our minds and, no doubt, was on the minds of the Twelve as well. No easy answers come. All humans are hostile to God and do not submit to him (Romans 8:7). We are flawed by sin and spiritually dead, unable to revive ourselves (Ephesians 2:1). When such hostile creatures come into contact with the gospel, some reject and oppose it. Those who believe marvel at the miracle God has worked within them. They take no credit for the change. It was not because they chose to believe and the others did not. It was not that they were somehow morally or spiritually superior to the others. It is altogether God's doing, or they would be like all the others who reject the gospel. The Word and the Spirit have done it, and we must stop there, perhaps a little confused at times, but we stop and marvel that God has made us his disciples.

Peter and the rest of the Twelve—save one—recognized that Jesus was the one who had come from above. He had confirmed that for them in the storm on the lake. When Jesus asked, "Do you want to go away as well?" Peter may have remembered the Lord's hand reaching out to him as he sank. The words of Jesus came to mind, including the words he had spoken to this crowd. So Peter answered, "Lord, to whom shall we go? You have the words of eternal life, and we have believed, and have come to know, that you are the Holy One of God."

Like Peter, we know Jesus has the words of eternal life and that he is the one who came to earth from heaven. His words are not the philosophies of human minds trying to make sense of this world. His words come from one who has seen God and has revealed God's deep love for fallen and imperfect people. "Everyone who looks on the Son and believes in him should have eternal life, and I will raise him up on the last day" (John 6:40). If Peter and the others were confused or harbored doubts, that one promise—that one truth—kept them close to Jesus. They wanted to hear the gracious words of life that came from him. But they didn't understand everything at this point. They didn't know exactly what Jesus meant when he said, "The bread that I will give for the life of the world is my flesh" (John 6:51). That would become clear only after the crucifixion and resurrection a year hence.

The sad and gloomy truth was that one of the Twelve did not hold to Peter's confession. Judas had seen Jesus reach for Peter on the sea. Judas had held one of the baskets filled with the leftovers from the feeding of the five thousand. He would yet see more, even the power of Jesus over death when Jesus raised Jairus' daughter and Lazarus. But Judas had placed something else ahead of Jesus and eternal life. It was not bread, as these people did. It was money. He had rejected the Word and all that it promised.

PRAYER: Lord, I am often confused with some unanswered questions about you and what you have revealed in the Scriptures. Draw me close to you when I have such doubts and confusion. Help me set them aside in the comforting truth that in all my uncertainty and misgivings, you have given me eternal life. May that be my treasure that I am unwilling by the power of the Holy Spirit to yield in the face of opposition, ridicule, and persecution. For the sake of your deep love for me. Amen.

16

Human Rules

Then Pharisees and scribes came to Jesus from Jerusalem and said, "Why do your disciples break the tradition of the elders? For they do not wash their hands when they eat." He answered them, "And why do you break the commandment of God for the sake of your tradition? For God commanded, 'Honor your father and your mother,' and, 'Whoever reviles father or mother must surely die.' But you say, 'If anyone tells his father or his mother, "What you would have gained from me is given to God," he need not honor his father.' So for the sake of your tradition you have made void the word of God. You hypocrites! Well did Isaiah prophesy of you, when he said: "'This people honors me with their lips, but their heart is far from me; in vain do they worship me, teaching as doctrines the commandments of men.'" And he called the people to him and said to them, "Hear and understand: it is not what goes into the mouth that defiles a person, but what comes out of the mouth; this defiles a person." (Matthew 15:1-11)

After the discussion about the Bread of Life, John writes that Jesus traveled in Galilee. He did not go south into Judea and Jerusalem "because the Jews were seeking to kill him" (John 7:1). He would, however, go to Jerusalem for the Feast of Booths in fall, about six months before his suffering and death. In addition, at times he would even disappear temporarily from Galilee and travel to out-of-the-way places to teach his disciples.

While he was in Galilee, he often had to deal with opposition coming north from Jerusalem. The Pharisees had challenged Jesus and his disciples earlier for picking grain and eating it on the Sabbath. Jesus had asserted his authority over the Sabbath laws, claiming to be "Lord of the Sabbath." He had also challenged the Pharisees in the synagogue by asking if it was lawful to do good on the Sabbath. He then healed the hand of a man in the synagogue. This also asserted Jesus' authority—not only a divine authority to heal but also the authority to use his divine power.

The challenge for most of the Jews came from their inability to accept that Jesus was more than an ordinary human being. His miracles had given them evidence that he was more. In the discussion with those who had eaten bread on the shore of the Sea of Galilee, Jesus more than once had said that he was the Bread of Life that had come from heaven. He could not have been more precise: "I have come down from heaven" (John 6:38). Because they knew the family of Jesus, they simply could not accept his assertion. "Is not this Jesus, the son of Joseph, whose father and mother we know? How does he now say, 'I have come down from heaven'?" (John 6:42).

One of the most frequently raised issues about Jesus over the past two thousand years is just that issue. How could Jesus—obviously a human who walked, talked, ate, and even cried—have come down from heaven? How could that be? Many of the heresies throughout history trace their origin to the difficulty to believe what Jesus said about himself. Many of our contemporary, everyday opinions about Jesus revolve around the same issue. By what right does Jesus tell us what to do, think, and believe? We will continue to encounter those who do not accept his divine authority to speak the truth we need to hear, believe, and act upon.

The Pharisees from Jerusalem approached the question from a little different direction. It was a question about their ancient traditions: "Why do your disciples break the tradition of the elders?" Their thinking was clear. The tradition of washing hands before eating stretched back to their revered elders. It was a good tradition. A healthy practice. But it was tied to all the other rituals and traditions that they believed honored God and showed true devotion to God's ways.

Jesus was not gentle with them. He identified a tradition that clearly violated the command of God. The Lord said to honor father and mother. But the traditions of the Pharisees said that if you had money to help your parents and you dedicated that money to God, you didn't have to use it to care for your parents. The brutal indictment came from the lips of Jesus: "You hypocrites!" Not only did they allow their traditions to excuse them from obeying God's commands, but they also believed that obeying the traditions made them pious and worthy of God's notice and favor.

The question here is really one of authority. How could Jesus teach and live differently than their revered elders? How could he be better than they were? How could he disregard their thoughts and rules? In other words, who does he think he is?

But Jesus deepened the lesson and challenged them to think that religion, piety, and devotion to God do not depend on outward deeds. Much of human thought is good. But human thought does not teach true worship of God. Human rules and traditions could not equal true worship of God. Jesus quoted from Isaiah, "In vain do they worship me, teaching as doctrines the commandments of men." God's truth was greater and should occupy their hearts. Mouths and lips could say all kinds of things—good and bad. Outward traditions—even when very beneficial—were not enough to curry God's favor. The heart that rested on God's promises was different.

Jesus made the point to the crowd. He invited the crowd to come closer. All the dietary regulations of the Jewish Torah and Talmud made the Jews distinctive in the world. Yet keeping certain foods out of their mouths and digestive systems did not free them from sin. Eating the foods forbidden in those dietary regulations did not defile them or make them unworthy. What makes them unworthy and defiles anyone is what comes out of the mouth. The language we use reveals what is inside—the sin we possess within. That defiles us. These Pharisees needed the forgiveness that cleanses inside and creates a new spirit that longs to serve God from the heart. So do we.

PRAYER: Lord Jesus, you have come down from heaven. I believe and confess you are "God from God, Light from Light, true God from true God" (Nicene Creed). Help me treasure you in my heart and listen to your Word because it is the Word from God for me and all humanity. When I am tempted to give the words of others more importance than your words, remind me not to follow "merely human rules." For your sake. Amen.

17

The Evil Within

Then the disciples came and said to [Jesus], "Do you know that the Pharisees were offended when they heard this saying?" He answered, "Every plant that my heavenly Father has not planted will be rooted up. Let them alone; they are blind guides. And if the blind lead the blind, both will fall into a pit." But Peter said to him, "Explain the parable to us." And he said, "Are you also still without understanding? Do you not see that whatever goes into the mouth passes into the stomach and is expelled? But what comes out of the mouth proceeds from the heart, and this defiles a person. For out of the heart come evil thoughts, murder, adultery, sexual immorality, theft, false witness, slander. These are what defile a person. But to eat with unwashed hands does not defile anyone." (Matthew 15:12-20)

It is almost as if the disciples had taken a page from a public relations textbook or seminar. They asked Jesus, "Do you know that the Pharisees were offended?" Perhaps it was the popularity of Jesus that sparked the question. The disciples were dedicated to Jesus, and they wanted to see the message they treasured reach as many people as possible. But Jesus had called the Pharisees hypocrites worshiping God in vain.

To their credit, the disciples came to Jesus with their question. But the question reveals a misplaced emphasis on what others thought. They had heard Jesus speak of eternal life to those who wanted to make him king. That was a hard saying and many walked away in confusion and disappointment. The disciples did not. Peter confessed, "You have the words of eternal life" (John 6:68). They remained at Jesus' side no matter how difficult the lesson may have been to understand.

The words of Jesus to the Pharisees are more difficult to understand. Why offend these devout and important leaders? Why use such sharp and judgmental words? Perhaps the disciples wondered why

Jesus had not minimized the tension and conflict with the Pharisees. Perhaps they felt a bit embarrassed by Jesus.

Jesus answers their questions by reminding them of the parables explaining the kingdom of God: the sower and the weeds. The disciples were the result of the sower's good seed. They had grown in their faith and become productive believers—not perfect, but still believers. Like them, believers in this world will never be perfect. They will always have questions and stumble along the way. But the disciples had found the priceless treasure and the pearl of great value—Jesus. They had cast their lot with Jesus.

But they lived in a world where not everyone had faith in Jesus and loyalty to his message. The parable of the weeds revealed that reality. The Pharisees did not believe that Jesus had come from heaven to give life. The incident with them was a practical example of the parable. Now Jesus makes the point clear. Those who did not believe would be pulled up by the roots just as the weeds had been at the harvest. But they were not to be uprooted now. Jesus said, "Leave them," echoing the words of the owner to his servants when they came wondering what to do about the weeds that had sprouted in the field. A time for judgment would come—a time for separation like the fish in a net that held good and bad fish. The good would be collected; the bad discarded. The judgment would come, but not now. Now the disciples were to sow seed.

One more point. Jesus identified the Pharisees as "blind guides." He sowed the seeds of the gospel just as he explained in the parables. He did not call down fire from heaven and destroy these critics who were seeking his death. But he did identify the danger they posed. They led others away with their blind unbelief. So Jesus was warning his disciples: Not everyone speaks positive and innocuous words about spiritual matters. Their task was to identify the false ideas and those who proclaimed them, but they were not to bring them into court or inflict harm or judgment upon them. This is a lesson for all believers who encounter not only opposition but also false teachings.

Peter wanted more explanation of the parable. Jesus was a little impatient with him: "Are you also still without understanding?" The picture Jesus used in his explanation is common and easy to understand.

What comes out of the body from eating and digesting is not pleasant. Then the lesson turned to spiritual truths. What comes out of a person's mouth flows from the heart. Those words often are not pleasant. Evil thoughts, murder, adultery, sexual immorality, theft, false testimony, and slander reside within the human heart. Words that flow from an evil heart defile a person.

The Pharisees had it wrong. They thought that they could avoid evil by following some dietary regulations and performing some sacrifice and by their public religious respectability including prayers and rituals. Those outward gestures could not purify the evil within. That is why they were blind. They did not see that a change of heart had to occur. Their inner person had to change before anything good could come out of their mouths and become part of their lives.

Jesus came to make that change within the human heart. He did it by love. He loved these disciples and all humanity enough to free them from their sinful hearts. His forgiveness changes people. He gives them a new heart, freed from the human blindness of thinking that outward habits and a godly exterior can make a person good. Those things only make a good-looking hypocrite who has not changed within.

What lessons we can learn here! The Word of God—the gospel—that announces God's love for sinners and his forgiveness changes people from the inside out. Yet not everyone believes and is changed. We are to continue to sow the seed of the gospel and identify false ideas as a warning for others lest they "fall into the pit." But we are not to uproot and destroy them. Leave them, Jesus said. Preach the gospel because it will change hearts and insert a new power—a new self—within.

PRAYER: Lord Jesus, your grace has changed me from the inside out and given me a new heart that desires to serve you and tell others about your grace and mercy to sinful humans. That change has also brought me hope for the glories of life with you forever. When I see and hear others who suggest that spiritual change comes from their outward activities, help me share the change you have created within me—a change they also can experience. If they object and are offended by your words of forgiveness, life, and salvation, keep me faithful to you and your gospel. Amen.

18

Son of David, Have Mercy on Me!

Jesus went away from there and withdrew to the district of Tyre and Sidon. And behold, a Canaanite woman from that region came out and was crying, "Have mercy on me, O Lord, Son of David; my daughter is severely oppressed by a demon." But he did not answer her a word. And his disciples came and begged him, saying, "Send her away, for she is crying out after us." He answered, "I was sent only to the lost sheep of the house of Israel." But she came and knelt before him, saying, "Lord, help me." And he answered, "It is not right to take the children's bread and throw it to the dogs." She said, "Yes, Lord, yet even the dogs eat the crumbs that fall from their masters' table." Then Jesus answered her, "O woman, great is your faith! Be it done for you as you desire." And her daughter was healed instantly. (Matthew 15:21-28)

Jesus withdrew from Gennesaret. Mark tells us that he entered a house in the region outside Jewish territory in Tyre and Sidon (Mark 7:24). He wanted to leave behind the Galilean crowds and the attempts of the Pharisees from Jerusalem to discredit him. We have no indication of the reason, but he wanted to keep his presence a secret, perhaps to find a quiet place to pray. He did that often. Sometimes he also took his disciples away from the constant interruptions of the crowd to spend time teaching them. They often came to Jesus with their questions at those times. The reason for withdrawing could be a combination of these thoughts. We just don't know for sure.

But even here away from Galilee, Mark writes, "he entered a house and did not want anyone to know, yet he could not be hidden" (7:24). A woman heard Jesus was there and abandoned caution to approach such a famous person. She was Greek, not a Galilean. She was clearly an outsider according to all Jewish standards. She came boldly, crying out loudly that she had a problem only Jesus could solve. Her daughter was afflicted—demon-possessed, the gospels say.

But there was more than just her bold and somewhat annoying cry for help. She called Jesus "Lord, Son of David." Her heart harbored faith in Jesus as the promised Messiah. Where had she heard of him? Who had planted the seed of the gospel? We have no answers, but the Holy Spirit had created faith within her. She had enough faith not just to address Jesus in the language of God's Old Testament prophecies but also to know that he had a heart filled with mercy for people in need. She came. She begged for mercy. She herself appeared to be possessed with her daughter's need and the hope of help from Jesus. The disciples found her annoying: "She is crying out after us."

Jesus did nothing. Not a word to her. Perhaps the disciples assumed that Jesus didn't want to be bothered, so they asked him to send her away. Then Jesus spoke, not a gentle, compassionate response but harsh and cold words: "I was sent only to the lost sheep of the house of Israel." True. Jesus was born in Bethlehem as a Jew. The Old Testament Scriptures foretold his coming and his work. He had even sent out his disciples and instructed them, "Go nowhere among the Gentiles and enter no town of the Samaritans, but go rather to the lost sheep of the house of Israel" (Matthew 10:5-6). "Send her away" was a logical request from the Twelve.

The prayers of the woman continued. She did not stop after the dismissive response of Jesus. She knelt before him and implored, "Lord, help me." But the response from Jesus was anything but encouraging: "It is not right to take the children's bread and throw it to the dogs." Dogs? Toss it? Ouch! No matter. She knew Jesus had the power to help. He was there, and she persisted.

She even demonstrated humility along with her deep faith in him. She turned the belittling label "dogs" into a desperate prayer. "Even the dogs eat the crumbs that fall from their master's table." She became a beggar at the feet of her Lord. She accepted her status. It was almost as if she became a pet dog and looked up at her master with imploring eyes. What absolute faith in him! What humility in her!

Jesus responded with a wonderful compliment and the answer to her prayers: "O woman, great is your faith! Be it done for you as you desire." Grace colors all of the Lord's dealings with her and with us. She was an outcast—not a daughter of Abraham but a Greek. She had nothing to offer Jesus. She proposed no bargain with him. Unworthy, an outcast, and deserving nothing, she received a gracious answer to her prayer.

Together with the Twelve we have much to learn. First, we need to come to the Lord with our prayers. He invites us to pray and promises to hear us. But sometimes he doesn't seem to care and seems to dismiss our heartrending requests. Persist! Persist like the woman. While we may not receive exactly what we request, he will give us what we need the most.

Second, faith trusts in the mercy of the Lord. Faith pleads. We understand who we are: lost, helpless sinners—beggars. The Lord has the love and power to do whatever he needs to do for our good. That's his promise and that's how we need to pray. His mercy gives us not what we deserve but what is undeserved. We too are foreigners—outcasts because of our birth and our sin. But the Lord treats us with grace and does not treat us as we deserve, as scavenger dogs that deserve to be kicked and shooed away. That's part of the lesson for us and the disciples.

In addition, the disciples needed to see beyond the horizon of Galilee and Judea. Here was a soul that trusted in the Son of David but was not of the lost sheep of Israel. Yet she was a dearly loved sheep who had heard the gospel and believed it. Some friend or some acquaintance or even some stranger had told this woman about Jesus. This lesson had a lasting impact. Later, the disciples would hear Jesus tell them, "Go therefore and make disciples of all nations" (Matthew 28:19).

The journey to the region of Tyre and Sidon was worth the lessons Jesus provided.

PRAYER: Lord, Son of David, hear my pleas for mercy. When I become impatient or am tempted to give up, hopeless of your help, strengthen my faith so that I continue my prayers. I deserve nothing from you, yet you have given me forgiveness and eternal life—gifts of grace. Help me remember that if you have given me these great blessings, you will also give me the lesser blessings that I need and that are good for me. As a humble beggar, I come pleading for mercy. Amen.

19

Be Opened!

Then [Jesus] returned from the region of Tyre and went through Sidon to the Sea of Galilee, in the region of the Decapolis. And they brought to him a man who was deaf and had a speech impediment, and they begged him to lay his hand on him. And taking him aside from the crowd privately, he put his fingers into his ears, and after spitting touched his tongue. And looking up to heaven, he sighed and said to him, "Ephphatha," that is, "Be opened." And his ears were opened, his tongue was released, and he spoke plainly. And Jesus charged them to tell no one. But the more he charged them, the more zealously they proclaimed it. And they were astonished beyond measure, saying, "He has done all things well. He even makes the deaf hear and the mute speak." (Mark 7:31-37)

The lesson at Tyre for the disciples was in the words of the woman seeking the help of Jesus: "Even the dogs under the table eat the children's crumbs" (Mark 7:28). Her humble perspective is more than a lesson in humility. She was not a Jew, a daughter of God's people, but an outsider—a Gentile. That distinction was part of the daily breath of the disciples. They were citizens of the nation that was awaiting the coming of the Messiah. Jesus had come, and they confessed him as the Messiah. Perhaps that was why they told Jesus to send the woman away. "She's not one of us," they thought. So they wanted to dismiss her.

But Jesus offered them another lesson. It came pointedly yet gently when Jesus healed her daughter. This miracle of Jesus began to move the disciples from their racial prejudices. The woman could also receive the Savior's love and merciful ministry. She was not to be excluded because she was not one of them.

Then Jesus left Tyre and Sidon. But note where he went: to the region of Decapolis (Ten Cities). Jesus and his disciples traveled from Tyre to this region on the eastern side of the Sea of Galilee and the Jordan River. The Ten Cities were independent city-states patterned after the Greeks. The people there had been liberated from Jewish rule by Pompey in 63 B.C. and based their calendar on that important date. They were a mixture of Greek, Roman, and Semitic peoples—certainly not Jewish. One of the cities was on the western side of the Jordan. Excavation of that site (Beth She'an) clearly reveals its Greek and Roman character.

So why go there? First, Jesus wanted to avoid the opposition of the Jewish leaders as he continued to instruct his disciples before his crucifixion. This was an area those leaders preferred to avoid. Second, Jesus was extending the important lesson they had just learned in Tyre. The benefits of his love were for all people, including those of a culture and race different from the Jewish culture that dominated the disciples and the crowds he attracted in Judea and Galilee.

What could have been clearer than the events in Decapolis? Matthew mentions the crowds from Decapolis following Jesus (Matthew 4:23-25). Now Jesus was visiting them. Among the people there, some brought a special case needing the Savior's love and power. This man was deaf and had difficulty speaking, perhaps a difficulty that made it hard to keep from drooling or spitting as he tried to talk.

Jesus responded in a unique way. He gave this man his personal, individual attention, taking him aside away from the crowd. He demonstrated complete understanding of the man's challenges. The man's ears could not process sound; Jesus put his fingers in them. The man's mouth expressed words only with difficulty and perhaps left his chin wet with spit. Jesus spat on the ground. Since the man could not hear, Jesus looked to heaven and drew this man's attention to the source of his help. Jesus' deep sigh demonstrated his own empathy for the man as well as the mercy of God in heaven. Finally, he said, "Be opened," and it was so.

Was the lesson lost on the disciples? It may not have developed deep roots yet. That would take time and divine direction. But it was a lesson the Magi hinted at as they came from far away to honor the newborn King of the Jews. It was a lesson of the Old Testament prophets. Isaiah had written, "Your gates shall be open continually; day and night they shall not be shut" (Isaiah 60:11). The sight of Jesus' crucifixion and resurrection were in Jerusalem, but they were never intended only for the Jews.

After his resurrection, Jesus told his Jewish disciples they would be his witnesses to the ends of the earth (Acts 1:8). As difficult as it was for them, they crossed borders and overcame racial and cultural barriers. Even the early church with its deep Jewish roots struggled when Gentiles became believers. The disciples had to put this lesson into practice and overcome their racial and cultural prejudices. By God's grace, they did as Jesus had directed and demonstrated.

We also have difficulty with this lesson. Our world is as diverse as it was when Jesus ascended. We have been culturally conditioned to think first in terms of people like us. Even in the United States, supposedly a melting pot of nationalities, racial and cultural barriers persist. We still have difficulty bridging those differences and prefer to remain in our own comfort zones. We need this lesson. The love of Jesus is not our parochial or exclusive treasure. "God so loved the world," Jesus said so clearly (John 3:16). But it is not so easy to imagine, think, and live this principle when the people next to us are so different.

PRAYER: Jesus, Savior of the nations, help me overcome my own prejudices and foibles and lovingly embrace those who believe in you but are different from me. Help me share the gospel with all people, no matter what cultural or racial barriers exist between us. Help me also to embrace and love the believers your grace has made disciples from all nations. For the sake of your all-encompassing love. Amen.

20

Four Thousand

In those days, when again a great crowd had gathered, and they had nothing to eat, [Jesus] called his disciples to him and said to them, "I have compassion on the crowd, because they have been with me now three days and have nothing to eat. And if I send them away hungry to their homes, they will faint on the way. And some of them have come from far away." And his disciples answered him, "How can one feed these people with bread here in this desolate place?" And he asked them, "How many loaves do you have?" They said, "Seven." And he directed the crowd to sit down on the ground. And he took the seven loaves, and having given thanks, he broke them and gave them to his disciples to set before the people; and they set them before the crowd. And they had a few small fish. And having blessed them, he said that these also should be set before them. And they ate and were satisfied. And they took up the broken pieces left over, seven baskets full. And there were about four thousand people. And he sent them away. And immediately he got into the boat with his disciples and went to the district of Dalmanutha. (Mark 8:1-10)

Mark follows the Savior's travel to Decapolis with this miracle and the words "In those days . . ." What an interesting idea. Some have concluded that this is another version of Jesus' miracle of feeding the five thousand. Others, myself included, suggest it is a different miracle. Mark reports both (Mark 6:35-44).

In this region where the Gentiles dominated, Jesus still attracted large crowds. Some of the Jewish minority in Decapolis had traveled to Galilee to listen to Jesus. Matthew tells us of the presence of people from Decapolis (Matthew 4:25) just before he tells us of the Savior's Sermon on the Mount. That was perhaps over a year earlier. Discussion of the sermon and Jesus by those returning home would have sparked interest in him when he arrived in Decapolis. No doubt, some in the region had come a long distance for an opportunity to see and hear Jesus on their turf.

Wherever Jesus was, the crowds found him. In this case, the people had been with Jesus for some time—three days. During that time, Jesus healed many and taught them. His message continued to amaze them as it had in Galilee. Luke notes, "All spoke well of him and marveled at the gracious words that were coming from his mouth" (Luke 4:22).

His message was a bit different for the gentile audience. In Bethsaida, when Jesus fed the five thousand, he engaged in an extended discussion about manna and bread from heaven. The Jews would have clearly understood the references to the Old Testament. Here in Decapolis, Jesus would also have spoken gracious words of God's love for them, his forgiveness, and the eternal life he promised. The gospel message would not have changed, but Jesus may not have been so "Jewish" here. Here I see him teaching as Paul described: "To the Jews I became as a Jew, in order to win Jews. . . . To those outside the law I became as one outside the law . . . that I might win those outside the law" (1 Corinthians 9:20-21). This was a part of the lesson for the Twelve, who would have to face a gentile world after Jesus' ascension.

Jesus emphasized the lesson when he expressed his compassion for these people. They had been with him for three days with nothing to eat. Sending them away would not be compassionate. He said, "If I send them away hungry to their homes, they will faint on the way." He did not ask the disciples to feed the crowd as he had near Bethsaida, another remote place. There the disciples had been concerned about the cost of providing food for the crowd. Here they were concerned because there was no place to find enough to feed the crowd.

But, of course, Jesus has the answer. He simply asked, "How many loaves do you have?" The disciples had prepared for the time away from shops where they could buy bread. After three days they still had seven loaves left. Now the scene in Bethsaida was repeated here. The crowd ate their fill and still had leftovers—seven basketfuls.

The Gentiles in Decapolis had the same need for food as the Jews. Jesus provides food for both. His message —the gospel—was for both, and his compassion for people had no racial boundaries. Yet Jesus could not remain here. His mission would take him to Jerusalem, where he would die for Jews and Gentiles and rise again to give all humanity victory over death.

Jesus sent the crowd away, and he and the disciples sailed to the region of Dalmanutha. We don't know for sure where that was, but the disciples had much to think and talk about as they traveled. Since Tyre, Jesus had demonstrated that his love and compassion were for all people. His power provided relief for those outside the borders of Judea and Galilee. He was the Son of David, but he came for all the world. We too have much to think about. As his disciples, we need to look beyond ourselves and see the needs of others, including those who are different from us. Jesus has broadened our horizons. We need to show compassion to all people and share the gospel with all people just as he did.

PRAYER: Dear Jesus, I treasure your compassion for me. Your gospel message has drawn me to you. Your compassion extends to all that troubles me and causes me pain and difficulty. So I come seeking your help. Lord, as you show me compassion in all my situations, help me find ways to help others when they face difficulties. Broaden my horizons to see all those in need, and guide me to help them as I am able. For your sake. Amen.

21

Opposition Persists

The Pharisees and Sadducees came, and to test him they asked him to show them a sign from heaven. He answered them, "When it is evening, you say, 'It will be fair weather, for the sky is red.' And in the morning, 'It will be stormy today, for the sky is red and threatening.' You know how to interpret the appearance of the sky, but you cannot interpret the signs of the times. An evil and adulterous generation seeks for a sign, but no sign will be given to it except the sign of Jonah." So he left them and departed. (Matthew 16:1-4)

For a little while, Jesus was free of the questions and challenges of the Pharisees. Yet their opposition did not disappear. Jesus was on the other side of the Sea of Galilee for a time. When Jesus left Decapolis behind, crossed the sea, and arrived once again on the Jewish side of the Sea of Galilee, the Pharisees were ready for his return. They went to him. Matthew tells us that the Sadducees went with them. That's a significant development.

Pharisees and Sadducees were on opposite ends of the religious and political spectrum. But they went to Jesus together. It doesn't seem that they suddenly set aside their differences of opinions about Jewish law and national politics. A more logical conclusion is that they set aside their differences to oppose Jesus. His ministry had gained widespread influence among ordinary people. Both Pharisees and Sadducees felt they were losing influence. The Pharisees had been the first to oppose Jesus. Now the Sadducees joined the effort to discredit him. In his absence in Tyre and Decapolis, they most likely agreed to disagree on all issues except Jesus.

They went to him wanting proof—a sign from heaven—that Jesus was who he claimed to be. From one perspective, it was a reasonable request. After the feeding of the five thousand, he had claimed to be from heaven (John 6:1-15), so they wanted a sign that validated his claim. But Jesus had already demonstrated his claim repeatedly in Galilee and even in Decapolis. His miracles were a visible, tangible sign that he was more than a part of a family from Nazareth. They rejected him because he claimed to be "anointed . . . to proclaim good news" (Luke 4:18). His baptism in the Jordan River had revealed his origin and verified his claim: "This is my beloved Son, with whom I am well pleased" (Matthew 3:17), the voice announced, as the dove descended from heaven. Were any of these Pharisees or Sadducees there? Had any of them seen any of his miracles? They must have missed all those events. "Show us proof," they said.

Jesus attacked their assumptions. As political and religious leaders, they had not read the "signs of the times." The ministry of Jesus had shaken their core beliefs. He had appeared as the Messiah promised by the prophets. He was an unexpected challenge to the status quo. Jesus seemed to challenge the policy of peaceful existence under Roman rule. For the Sadducees, he posed a challenge to their political power and their belief that there is no resurrection—Jesus raised the dead. For the Pharisees, he was a challenge to the strict interpretation of the Mosaic Law and the traditions they held dear. No wonder both parties joined forces against him.

Although the signs from heaven were plentiful and powerful, Jesus did not give them another sign here. Even that would not have convinced them because their opposition had hardened into concrete. They were "an evil and adulterous generation," as Jesus said. Jesus had already given the Pharisees the sign of Jonah when they had asked for a sign (Matthew 12:38-45). He told them, "Just as Jonah was three days and three nights in the belly of the great fish, so will the Son of Man be three days and three nights in the heart of the earth" (Matthew 12:40).

The crucifixion and resurrection of Jesus—Good Friday and Easter—were signs that he was the Messiah. Later, when the Pharisees and Sadducees met to consider the empty tomb, would they remember what Jesus had said about Jonah? Jesus gave them words now to consider later. Would any of them be convinced? Some of them would indeed be convinced. Joseph of Arimathea and Nicodemus would remember and were strengthened in their faith. Some others might have come to believe, but many did not. After Easter morning, they devised the story that the disciples came and stole the body. They also protected the guards at the tomb from punishment for dereliction of duty—a serious charge for Roman soldiers.

The resurrection of Jesus is still the proof Jesus gives to the world that rejects him. If the Pharisees and Sadducees did not believe Jesus rose from the dead, they had to deal with those who saw Jesus. They noticed the dramatic transformation of the disciples from Galilean fishermen to bold evangelists. When we face those who reject Jesus, we can do no better than Jesus. We can point to the resurrection and conclude that those who do not believe are "an evil and adulterous generation" that will not believe any proof. The Scriptures are filled with proof that Jesus has come from heaven to bring us forgiveness and eternal life.

When Jesus spoke of the sign of Jonah, it was a clear indication that he had not forgotten about his suffering, death, and resurrection in Jerusalem. That was still in the future, but each day it grew closer.

PRAYER: Jesus, you have come from heaven and called me to be your disciple here at this time and in this place. You have completed my redemption by your suffering, death, and resurrection. You have also made known the will of your heavenly Father so that "everyone who looks on the Son and believes in him should have eternal life" (John 6:40). Help me hold fast to this truth when I am called names and ridiculed for my faith. Give me the courage to share the great hope I have in your resurrection from the dead. Amen.

22

Guard Against Yeast

When the disciples reached the other side, they had forgotten to bring any bread. Jesus said to them, "Watch and beware of the leaven of the Pharisees and Sadducees." And they began discussing it among themselves, saying, "We brought no bread." But Jesus, aware of this, said, "O you of little faith, why are you discussing among yourselves the fact that you have no bread? Do you not yet perceive? Do you not remember the five loaves for the five thousand, and how many baskets you gathered? Or the seven loaves for the four thousand, and how many baskets you gathered? How is it that you fail to understand that I did not speak about bread? Beware of the leaven of the Pharisees and Sadducees." Then they understood that he did not tell them to beware of the leaven of bread, but of the teaching of the Pharisees and Sadducees. (Matthew 16:5-12)

Jesus left the Pharisees and Sadducees. Perhaps these critics returned to Jerusalem licking their wounds from the harsh words of Jesus, but they weren't finished with him. Their opposition only grew more determined when Jesus had not been frightened or intimidated by their opposition. But Jesus was determined to continue his ministry until the end. So Jesus and his disciples left and went across the lake.

Why did Jesus persist in the face of such determined opposition? Why didn't he just leave, adopt a low profile, and seek safety? Why didn't he go back to Decapolis, far away from the Pharisees? Or perhaps travel east to other countries? Earlier he could have boarded a ship in Tyre and sailed anywhere in the Mediterranean. But he came back knowing he would confront the opposition again in the months ahead. Why?

The opposition would get stiffer. It would turn to anger and eventually succeed in getting Jesus arrested and crucified. Jesus knew that.

He told his disciples it would happen. Why come back to confront the Pharisees again and again? It was because he had a mission to fulfill. His heavenly Father had sent him to suffer and die in the place of all sinners so that all sinners like us, his disciples, and even the Pharisees would have forgiveness and eternal life. There was no one else to do that but Jesus. So he came back to redeem all humanity and cleanse the world by his blood (2 Corinthians 5:19; 1 John 1:7).

We, of course, would most likely take a different direction when facing opposition. We would hide out and refuse to engage the critics. We might prefer instead to sit quietly and listen to Jesus or remember better days. No doubt the disciples appreciated their respite from the constant hostility and antagonism that pursued them in these months. Perhaps they longed for the days of popularity—the miracles that were so universally appreciated and the crowds that flocked to hear Jesus.

But those days of acclaim and warm acceptance were slipping away. Yes, in Decapolis it was different; Jesus did not face the harsh critics of his ministry and mission. But after leaving Decapolis behind and returning to Galilee, there were the Pharisees and Sadducees. Jesus did not hide, and neither can we expect to hide out and avoid opposition and hostility. That might happen temporarily, but the gospel is always opposed, and we too will hear and read of those who think Jesus is unimportant. We may also face their hostility personally and feel the pain of opposition. We are no different from the disciples or our Master, Jesus.

One of the lessons Jesus taught the disciples during this time was to continue to sow the gospel. Jesus demonstrated that in Galilee early, in the parable of the sower, in Decapolis, and here on the western shores of the Sea of Galilee. They still had much to learn about sowing the seed of the gospel. Now was the time for another lesson.

Jesus warned them against the yeast of the Pharisees and Sadducees. The disciples did not understand at first. The feeding of the four thousand was still fresh in their memory, and they focused on bread. Perhaps they were worried that they had no bread left to give to Jesus if he should feed another crowd. They had provided the seven loaves, but now they had none. But this was not about them, the bread they did or didn't have, or even their failure to be prepared for the next event in their journey with Jesus.

It was about the truth. The message of Jesus was different from the message of the Pharisees and Sadducees. Jesus spoke of God's grace, his work of redeeming the world, and faith in him. Jesus had made that abundantly clear after the feeding of the five thousand (John 6). The message of the Jewish leaders was to follow the rules of the Mosaic Law and the traditions of the elders in order to gain God's approval. Their teachings were like a yeast that worked its way through the entire thought process of the disciples and distorted the free and undeserved grace of God toward sinners in Jesus.

Beware of that subtle influence. We have seen, read, and heard how some have made salvation depend on what humans do or don't do. The common religion of our age is the thinking of the Pharisees: When you are a good person and do good things for others, then God will be good to you. The yeast of earning God's love by our behavior distorts grace. No wonder Jesus warns, "Watch and beware." What a tragedy to desire to serve God like the Pharisees by keeping all the regulations but to lose the grace of God in all the effort, counting on your good effort instead of God's undeserved love for you.

PRAYER: Lord Jesus, I praise you for your resolve to complete the redemption of humanity you came to accomplish. I also ask that you keep me away from the influences of those who think they can earn your love by what they do. May I always trust that it is by grace I have been saved—not by works. Amen.

23

Gradual Sight

They came to Bethsaida. And some people brought to [Jesus] a blind man and begged him to touch him. And he took the blind man by the hand and led him out of the village, and when he had spit on his eyes and laid his hands on him, he asked him, "Do you see anything?" And he looked up and said, "I see people, but they look like trees, walking." Then Jesus laid his hands on his eyes again; and he opened his eyes, his sight was restored, and he saw everything clearly. And he sent him to his home, saying, "Do not even enter the village." (Mark 8:22-26)

Jesus wanted to separate his disciples from the Pharisees and Sadducees. So he and his disciples crossed the Sea of Galilee again and landed on the northern shore where Jesus had fed the five thousand before heading to Decapolis. Most likely, he would not return to Decapolis. He would spend some important time with his disciples and eventually make a couple of significant journeys to Jerusalem. His passion was less than a year away. And before that happened, Jesus needed to help his disciples understand what was going to happen. The lessons that Jesus taught his disciples now required some quiet time away from the constant attacks of his critics.

He and the disciples came to the northern shore and entered the village of Bethsaida. From what Mark implies, the crowds had not discovered that Jesus was there. Only "some people" from the village recognized him, and they asked Jesus to touch the blind man and heal him.

If Jesus was determined to travel farther north, he did not want to stop and draw attention to his presence. But he could not completely avoid the people of the village and their requests for help. His compassion for people was always evident. But in this case, the way Jesus handled the healing seems to indicate only a short stay in Bethsaida and a desire not to draw a crowd of people curious to see him.

When the family brought the blind man, Jesus took him by the hand and led him outside the village. This miracle is unique. It is not unique that Jesus spits to perform the miracle. He had done that in Decapolis (Mark 7:33) and would do it again later in Jerusalem (John 9:6). But what is unique about this miracle is that the man's sight came in two stages. After Jesus spit on the man's eyes, he asked, "Do you see anything?" The man did not see clearly, but he saw people who looked "like trees, walking." Jesus put his hands on the man's eyes, and this time the man saw clearly.

Why did this man receive sight gradually? Bible commentators either ignore the question or suggest a variety of answers. We simply do not know why Jesus chose to heal in this way. Was it because he and his disciples were on their way to Caesarea Philippi in the north? He had taken the man away from the village to heal him, perhaps choosing not to attract a crowd that would delay their journey. Then, since Jesus would not spend time teaching here, the gradual healing would make a deep impression on the man and emphasize the importance of Jesus.

Was it a lesson for the disciples? With some of the lessons later, Jesus would clarify why he had come. He would spend the next month telling them of his suffering, death, and resurrection in Jerusalem. They would have difficulty understanding that lesson. Was this man's gradual return to sight an object lesson for the disciples? They too did not have a clear vision of what Jesus had come to accomplish. At this point they saw Jesus as helper, miracle worker, and teacher holding out the promises of God (John 6:68) but did not see the full picture yet. Was Jesus teaching them that he had more to share with them so they could see clearly?

Peter wrote about the lessons he learned from Jesus. He spoke of the disciples being "eyewitnesses of his majesty" (2 Peter 1:16) and urged his readers to pay attention to Jesus' message "as to a lamp shining in a dark place, until the day dawns and the morning star rises in your hearts" (2 Peter 1:19). The light gradually dawned in Peter. In just a few days he would rebuke Jesus after Jesus said that he would suffer, be killed, and rise again. Even later, Peter would deny Jesus and stand dumbfounded before the empty tomb. But the light did finally come.

Are we any different? At times we have fuzzy ideas about Jesus. Do we sometimes think of him as someone who will heal and protect us from all harm? Do we sometimes think that Jesus should make our world calm and peaceful but then it isn't? We will experience pain and disease, trouble and trial. We will die. Jesus is not a miracle worker to keep us safe from every trial. He is the one who suffered and died so that we can be forgiven and justified before God. He rose again and gives us victory over death. Sometimes we see and understand these things gradually, recognizing that our vision of Jesus may be vague, like seeing people walking around like trees.

But Jesus gives us the clear picture—the full understanding of why he came. When we are confused and weak, we should return to Jesus and the message he taught his disciples so that when darkness threatens us and clouds our thinking, the message of Jesus will dawn as the morning light and rise in our hearts, leaving us with clarity about why Jesus came and how deeply he loves us. His cross and empty tomb make everything clear.

Why did Jesus tell the man not to return to the village? Jesus told him to go home but not to go back into the village. This was not the time for a crowd to gather after a miracle. It was a time for this man to think about Jesus and his power to heal. It was a time for gradual growth and reflection.

PRAYER: Jesus, you have given me the light of your love, but at times I stumble in the darkness of sin, doubt, and trial. At those times, shine in my heart with the love that brought you to the cross for me. Let the brightness of your empty tomb light my every step in this dark world. Amen.

24

You Are the Messiah!

When Jesus came into the district of Caesarea Philippi, he asked his disciples, "Who do people say that the Son of Man is?" And they said, "Some say John the Baptist, others say Elijah, and others Jeremiah or one of the prophets." He said to them, "But who do you say that I am?" Simon Peter replied, "You are the Christ, the Son of the living God." And Jesus answered him, "Blessed are you, Simon Bar-Jonah! For flesh and blood has not revealed this to you, but my Father who is in heaven. And I tell you, you are Peter, and on this rock I will build my church, and the gates of hell shall not prevail against it. I will give you the keys of the kingdom of heaven, and whatever you bind on earth shall be bound in heaven, and whatever you loose on earth shall be loosed in heaven." Then he strictly charged the disciples to tell no one that he was the Christ. (Matthew 16:13-20)

Jesus told the blind man not to return to the village but to go directly home. No large and curious crowd of people gathered about Jesus. They did not have time to bring their sick and lame, expecting other miracles. From Bethsaida and the miracle there, Jesus and the disciples continued their journey north. It was a quiet walk to Caesarea Philippi—a time for leisurely conversation along the way. They walked on without crowds or the sniping critics from Jerusalem that had dogged them in Galilee.

They walked for over 20 miles. Mark tells us they reached the villages of Caesarea Philippi but says nothing about any miracles or crowds there. Perhaps the mention of the villages is enough to indicate the intent of Jesus. His goal was to teach his disciples, not to prove his power and authority by miracles or by teaching the crowds. In other places the people were amazed at both his miracles and the power of his teaching. Here his focus was the disciples. He spent the time preparing them for his suffering, death, and resurrection in Jerusalem and the time when they would be his witnesses to the world.

So Jesus brought the disciples to Caesarea and continued their lessons with an important question: "Who do people say that the Son of Man is?" Their responses came from their conversations with others, what they had overheard, and perhaps also some of their own thoughts. They said that some concluded that Jesus was a reappearance of John the Baptist, whom Herod had beheaded. The other answers put Jesus in the company of the Old Testament prophets. Some believed that one of those prophets had come back to life, naming two: Elijah and Jeremiah. The people who had seen and heard Jesus knew that he was someone special even if they weren't exactly sure about his identity.

Jesus was not asking for an impersonal assessment of what the crowds thought. He asked pointedly, "Who do you say that I am?" They had followed Jesus from the early days in Galilee. They had listened and watched. They had heard the critics and how Jesus had responded. Peter was ready to respond for himself and for the others, "You are the Christ, the Son of the living God."

Peter had listened when Jesus engaged in the dialogue about the Bread of Life after the feeding of the five thousand. The Jews had grumbled when Jesus claimed to be the bread that came down from heaven. Jesus, who was from above, clearly promised a gift only God could deliver: "Everyone who looks on the Son and believes in him should have eternal life, and I will raise him up on the last day" (John 6:40). Then Peter recognized that Jesus was the only source of life and confessed, "We have believed, and have come to know, that you are the Holy One of God" (John 6:69).

How many other miracles had Peter and the others witnessed? How many words had they heard from Jesus in private and in public before the crowds who so eagerly listened and the critics who so quickly found reason to object? Peter wasn't the only one of the disciples to think this way. He may have been the first to say it, but they had all seen the same miracles and found in Jesus the fulfillment of all the Scripture's prophecies. Yes, he was the Messiah.

Peter and the others had not come to that conclusion on their own. Jesus called him blessed and gave him the name Peter, the rock, because what he had just confessed had been revealed to him by his Father in heaven. The seed Jesus had sown had sprouted by the power of God and grown into a bold faith. Jesus looked at Peter, complimented him on his faith, and then said he would build his church on the Messiah, the bedrock, whom Peter had just confessed. Peter was one stone among other apostles, but Jesus was the foundational stone of all believers, the church. To think that Peter was the bedrock is a mistake. Just how great a mistake would be evident in the next exchange between Jesus and his disciples.

The disciples had taken a huge step forward in acknowledging Jesus as the Messiah. But they did not yet understand all of what that meant. It meant more than miracles and lessons about God's truth. It meant more than friendly conversation with the Holy One of God along the road in the beautiful setting of Caesarea Philippi. If they began to proclaim that Jesus was the Messiah, confusion and conflict would come and make the months ahead more difficult. So Jesus told them not to tell anyone what they confessed at this time. The lessons they needed to learn would unfold soon.

PRAYER: Jesus, you are the Messiah, the Son of the living God. Help me always keep you and you alone as the foundation stone of my faith. You have completed your mission to die for my sins and rise again to give me eternal life. Give me strength to sow the seed of your gospel so that others may come to confess you as their foundation amid all of life's storms. Amen.

25

Why I Have Come

From that time Jesus began to show his disciples that he must go to Jerusalem and suffer many things from the elders and chief priests and scribes, and be killed, and on the third day be raised. And Peter took him aside and began to rebuke him, saying, "Far be it from you, Lord! This shall never happen to you." But he turned and said to Peter, "Get behind me, Satan! You are a hindrance to me. For you are not setting your mind on the things of God, but on the things of man." (Matthew 16:21-23)

Peter spoke for all the disciples when he confessed that Jesus was the Messiah, the Anointed One, the Christ. But none of them understood exactly what that meant. Jesus had strictly told them not to tell anyone that he was the Messiah. It was not the time to do that. They didn't understand it all, and telling others that Jesus was the Messiah would compound their misunderstanding as well as confirm and embolden those who thought Jesus was a false prophet. Imagine how the Pharisees would seize on this claim and raise havoc for Jesus and anyone who followed him. The situation was bad enough already. Sharing the news of Jesus being the Messiah at this time would have made it worse.

Jesus took one more step to help his disciples—one important lesson they still needed time to fully grasp. They were students of the Scriptures and understood that the prophets had foretold the coming of the Messiah. But some thought the Messiah would be a political or military leader to restore the glory of Israel by sweeping away the Romans. Simon the Zealot was among them, and he was one of the Twelve. Other ideas ranged from a political restoration to some kind of kingdom without disease and trouble, including a kingdom of peace and love that was vague enough to capture everyone's latent hopes. The

Messiah would usher in a great dramatic change, at least that's what the prophets had foretold, but most people, including the disciples, did not understand what that meant.

Jesus began to clarify what the Messiah would do: The Messiah had come to suffer, die, and rise to life again. That thought brought brutal and painful thoughts to all of the disciples. The one they loved and followed would "suffer many things from the elders and chief priests and scribes." How could that be? Why was that to happen? On one level, they understood the opposition of the Jewish leaders. But to imagine that opposition would bring about such a bloody outcome was difficult.

Peter, as bold and rash as ever, took Jesus aside and "began to rebuke him." It's difficult to imagine Peter, who had just identified Jesus as the Messiah, rebuking the one whom God had sent into the world—the Anointed One. Who did he think he was? Is there any wonder that Jesus had decided not to build his church on Peter? Jesus was the best—the only— foundation for the church that could withstand the forces of hell itself.

"This shall never happen to you," Peter said. He did not want to see the suffering and death of the one he deeply loved. He and the others said they were willing to die before they would let anything happen to Jesus. Near the end of Jesus' ministry, when he led the disciples toward Jerusalem, Andrew told the others, "Let us also go, that we may die with him" (John 11:16). Even then they did not understand fully what was going to happen and what it meant. Here Jesus strongly challenges Peter, calling him Satan. Peter had set himself and his thinking against the concerns of God. He let his human affection cloud his thinking. He did not understand.

But Jesus clearly understood. His mission had been set before he was born. His heavenly Father sent him to take the place of every human sinner; suffer for their faults, failures, and sins; and overcome death for them. He resolutely accepted his task. It was fast approaching, and his disciples needed to have at least some idea of why Jesus, the Messiah, had come.

Yet it was fuzzy in the minds of all the disciples now. Jesus would painstakingly continue to tell them what was to happen. This was the beginning. After it had all happened, they would understand. Even Peter would understand. He would write,

> Knowing that you were ransomed from the futile ways inherited from your forefathers, not with perishable things such as silver or gold, but with the precious blood of Christ, like that of a lamb without blemish or spot. He was foreknown before the foundation of the world but was made manifest in the last times for the sake of you who through him are believers in God, who raised him from the dead and gave him glory, so that your faith and hope are in God. (1 Peter 1:18-21)

Gradually it would all fall into place.

PRAYER: Lord, I often think that I know better and more than you do and challenge your truth and wonder why you do things as you do. Forgive me for my bold and insolent arrogance. Keep me as a humble student of your Word rather than an arrogant teacher of what I do not fully understand. As a humble student, keep me from abandoning the forgiveness, life, peace, and joy you have come to give me as the Messiah sent to earth. Amen.

26

Take Up Your Cross

Then Jesus told his disciples, "If anyone would come after me, let him deny himself and take up his cross and follow me. For whoever would save his life will lose it, but whoever loses his life for my sake will find it. For what will it profit a man if he gains the whole world and forfeits his soul? Or what shall a man give in return for his soul? For the Son of Man is going to come with his angels in the glory of his Father, and then he will repay each person according to what he has done. Truly, I say to you, there are some standing here who will not taste death until they see the Son of Man coming in his kingdom." (Matthew 16:24-28)

When Jesus began to tell his disciples about the suffering, death, and resurrection that awaited him, Peter had rebuked him: "Far be it from you, Lord! This shall never happen to you" (Matthew 16:22). Rebuke Jesus? What was Peter thinking? Jesus called Peter "Satan" and identified what he was thinking: "You are not setting your mind on the things of God, but on the things of man" (Matthew 16:23). It was time for another lesson. This time the lesson was what it meant to be a disciple of Jesus.

Mark tells us that Jesus invited the crowd to join the disciples before he spoke. His words were startling and memorable. "If anyone would come after me, let him deny himself and take up his cross and follow me." This lesson is recorded also in the gospels of Mark and Luke, so it made a deep impression. But what did it mean?

Peter's rebuke in Matthew chapter 16 gives us some idea of what denying yourself means. As Jesus said, Peter had his mind on "things of man." When Peter rebuked Jesus, he revealed the flaw in the human spirit. The sinful human heart wants only what it thinks is good for itself. It is sinful and does not want what God wants. It sees no need for the suffering, death, and resurrection of Jesus. "This shall never happen to you," Peter said (Matthew 16:22). Our natures oppose God too. We are rebels against God.

The sinful nature rejects God's plan. It is perverse and wants to live outside of God's will in every way. It is the self that says, "I know better than God." That attitude is part of our everyday life and shows up in our thinking about how good we are, how deserving we are of God's care, and even how deserving we are of heaven. Jesus explained what that human effort means: When we want to save our life on our own, we will lose it.

Jesus directs disciples to deny themselves, to turn away from the dead end of our own thinking and effort. You cannot find life there. Being a disciple means denying the human idea of entering heaven with the passport of your good efforts, good intentions, or kindnesses and generosity. Deny every inclination to think that way. Deny every urge to find a way around his will and excuse disobedience to his commands.

Denying yourself is a part of repentance. It's turning away from the sinful nature within and denying its control. Repentance is also turning toward something else: God's grace in Christ, his suffering, death, and resurrection—his cross. There we find life. We know the Son of Man and understand the glory he promised his disciples in the presence of his Father's glory.

When we deny ourselves, we have a changed perspective. Disciples are transformed by God's grace. Turning away from sin and trusting in Jesus means that disciples have found the greatest treasure and are ready to hold on to it at all costs—to take up their cross.

But taking up the cross is not easy. It means a constant struggle with the sinful flesh. It means enduring opposition, ridicule, and persecution rather than laying down the cross to seek safety and life here. It means quieting the questions that suffering here creates in our weak hearts with the assurance that the reward is real and waiting for us. It means opposing the natural inclination to blame God and abandon the cross. We endure the crosses of Christian living. Disciples are ready to follow Jesus wherever he leads and endure every obstacle that would turn them away from his promises.

Taking up the cross was a lesson for Peter and all the disciples as they went forward. Jesus would teach them the lesson again by his actions and words as he fulfilled the prediction he had just shared with the Twelve. He too had a cross. He remained obedient to his heavenly Father no matter what suffering he had to endure, including crucifixion. His cross would achieve a reward for all his disciples—a reward fully paid for by his pain, blood, and death.

Jesus spoke of the cross in the area of Caesarea, which was named after Roman emperors and dominated by Roman influences. The word Jesus uses—*cross*—would come into focus again later. When Jesus was nailed to a Roman cross in Jerusalem, these words came back into the disciples' heads and hearts. They watched Jesus carry his cross and, quite likely, remembered him saying that discipleship meant carrying their own crosses.

So Jesus reminds them of the glory to come. He speaks of the Son of Man coming in his kingdom. Some standing in the crowd on this day would not taste death before they saw the Son of Man coming in his kingdom. They would see not only his death and resurrection but also his ascension and the miracle of Pentecost. They needed this lesson and the promise of Jesus now. The fulfillment of those promises in Jerusalem made them ready to pick up their crosses. His promises gave them strength when they stood before a crowd in Jerusalem and boldly proclaimed Jesus crucified and risen again. They would endure the persecution that came. Deny yourself. Take your cross. Follow Jesus.

PRAYER: Lord Jesus, you took up your cross that was weighted with my sins and the sins of the world. You were bruised and punished for my sins. You have bought and purchased my reward and that of all people with your suffering, death, and resurrection. By your grace I have listened to your invitation and gladly follow you. Keep me faithful to you and give me the power to bear whatever crosses I must until I join you in your glorious, eternal kingdom. Amen.

27

The Transfiguration

After six days Jesus took with him Peter and James, and John his brother, and led them up a high mountain by themselves. And he was transfigured before them, and his face shone like the sun, and his clothes became white as light. And behold, there appeared to them Moses and Elijah, talking with him. And Peter said to Jesus, "Lord, it is good that we are here. If you wish, I will make three tents here, one for you and one for Moses and one for Elijah." He was still speaking when, behold, a bright cloud overshadowed them, and a voice from the cloud said, "This is my beloved Son, with whom I am well pleased; listen to him." When the disciples heard this, they fell on their faces and were terrified. But Jesus came and touched them, saying, "Rise, and have no fear." And when they lifted up their eyes, they saw no one but Jesus only. And as they were coming down the mountain, Jesus commanded them, "Tell no one the vision, until the Son of Man is raised from the dead." (Matthew 17:1-9)

Both Matthew and Mark place Jesus and the disciples in Caesarea Philippi when Jesus asked, "Who do people say that the Son of Man is?" (Matthew 16:13). The disciples and the people had turned to Scripture for potential answers. Because they were in Caesarea, another answer may have come to mind. Herod the Great had built a magnificent temple and dedicated it to Caesar, the Roman emperor. Then Herod's son Philip enlarged the area and honored not only the new Caesar but also the nature god Pan. It was called Caesarea Philippi to distinguish it from Caesarea, which was to the west on the shore of the Mediterranean. The area was a kind of nature preserve with a temple and shrine for the god Pan. The Jordan River began its southern journey to the Dead Sea from a cave there. The place was clearly not Jewish but pagan and Roman.

Farther north stood Mount Hermon, stretching over 9,000 feet toward the sky and sometimes boasting snow in the brilliant sunshine. Here too was an emphasis on pagan deities. Jesus reminded his disciples that he was not a prophet brought back to life. Nor was he the incarnation of some pagan god. In this beautiful setting with all its pagan influences, Peter had confessed that Jesus was the Christ, the Son of the living God.

Then Jesus taught another important lesson to the disciples. He chose to share the lesson with only three of the disciples and gave explicit instructions not to share the lesson with the others until "the Son of Man is raised from the dead." The lesson began with a private walk with Peter, James, and John to a high mountain. Jesus had told them that some would not see death until they saw the kingdom of God come with power. But Jesus had also told the disciples that he would suffer, be killed, and rise again. Perhaps they were confused, but Peter, James, and John followed Jesus up the mountain.

Then, suddenly, Jesus was transfigured! His clothing was dazzling white, whiter than the snow on Mount Hermon or than anyone could bleach them. This lesson identified Jesus as "the Son of the living God" (Matthew 16:16), as Peter and the disciples confessed, but more. Elijah and Moses were standing with Jesus. He was the Christ, the Messiah, sent from heaven. Elijah had been greeted by a chariot of fire and carried to heaven in a whirlwind. Moses had seen God "face to face" (Exodus 33:11), and his face had become glorified after his conversations with God. There both Elijah and Moses stood "talking with [Jesus]."

It was awe-inspiring, and Peter was struck with its splendor. He wanted to build three shelters there. Perhaps he was thinking of the shrines they may have seen in Caesarea or on the journey to the mountain. Shrines commemorate such events and, like the shrine of Pan in Caesarea, drew people to a specific place in order to give homage to an event or person or god. Certainly, Jesus and this event deserved such homage.

But before Peter could pick up stones to mark the spot or even get an answer to his request to build, a bright cloud appeared and covered them. They were suddenly included in the vision with Jesus, Elijah, and Moses. A voice spoke, "This is my beloved Son, with whom I am well pleased; listen to him." The voice confirmed the confession of Peter and the others that Jesus was "the Christ, the Son of the living God" (Matthew 16:16). But the voice also dispelled the idea of creating a shine there. "Listen to him," the voice from the cloud said. No shrine here or anywhere. Just listen to the Messiah as Elijah and Moses had.

Then there they stood with Jesus. The cloud, Moses, and Elijah were gone. Peter, James, and John had seen the kingdom of God that stretched from the Old Testament prophets to Jesus and to them. It was one kingdom with Jesus at its center, and it included them. The kingdom was not built on Peter. And it was not to be a shrine for pilgrimage, reverence, or some mystical connection with what happened there. The kingdom clearly came through the words of Jesus, "Listen to him," and those who listened would be included in the kingdom.

Jesus then told them not to say anything until his crucifixion and resurrection had occurred. If they had told the others, they might have wanted to do what Peter wanted to do: build a shrine there. But greater glories—all tied to the suffering, death, and resurrection of Jesus—were to come. They would see the kingdom of God come in glory when Jesus burst from the tomb. They would see the glory of the kingdom when the Holy Spirit descended as fire on their heads at Pentecost. Then they would see the kingdom come and enfold others who came to faith in Jesus through the words Jesus had taught them.

PRAYER: Lord Jesus, you have given me your words through the apostles, who were eyewitnesses of your glory and who not only listened to your words but also wrote them down for all. Keep my ears open to your words. Focus my attention on your suffering, death, and resurrection and not on the places you walked and visited, lest I be drawn away from the great blessings of your cross and empty tomb. Amen.

28

Down to Earth Again

When they came to the disciples, they saw a great crowd around them, and scribes arguing with them. And immediately all the crowd, when they saw him, were greatly amazed and ran up to him and greeted him. And he asked them, "What are you arguing about with them?" And someone from the crowd answered him, "Teacher, I brought my son to you, for he has a spirit that makes him mute. And whenever it seizes him, it throws him down, and he foams and grinds his teeth and becomes rigid. So I asked your disciples to cast it out, and they were not able." And he answered them, "O faithless generation, how long am I to be with you? How long am I to bear with you? Bring him to me." And they brought the boy to him. And when the spirit saw him, immediately it convulsed the boy, and he fell on the ground and rolled about, foaming at the mouth. And Jesus asked his father, "How long has this been happening to him?" And he said, "From childhood. And it has often cast him into fire and into water, to destroy him. But if you can do anything, have compassion on us and help us." And Jesus said to him, "'If you can'! All things are possible for one who believes." Immediately the father of the child cried out and said, "I believe; help my unbelief!" And when Jesus saw that a crowd came running together, he rebuked the unclean spirit, saying to it, "You mute and deaf spirit, I command you, come out of him and never enter him again." And after crying out and convulsing him terribly, it came out, and the boy was like a corpse, so that most of them said, "He is dead." But Jesus took him by the hand and lifted him up, and he arose. And when he had entered the house, his disciples asked him privately, "Why could we not cast it out?" And he said to them, "This kind cannot be driven out by anything but prayer." (Mark 9:14-29)

Jesus, Peter, James, and John came down from the mountain. The glorious vision of Jesus and the warm voice of the Father encouraging them to listen to Jesus were locked in their memory. Peter mentions it in his second letter. "We were eyewitnesses of his majesty" (2 Peter 1:16). What a memory! What a treasure!

What greeted them when they returned was not majestic, glorious, or encouraging. They found a large crowd, and Mark tells us that the teachers of the law were arguing with the disciples who had remained at the base of the mountain. Even worse, they were arguing because the disciples could not heal a father's afflicted son. The disciples had failed. It was a heart-wrenching case. The son had seizures and had suffered greatly since his birth. The father pleaded with Jesus to "have compassion on [them] and help [them.]" What made this scene all the more ominous was that Satan was on the prowl. The child was plagued by an evil spirit. Satan lurked here to disrupt, discredit, and destroy so much.

Jesus saw the conflict, failure, heartache, and danger. But he also saw unbelief. The teachers of the law thought they had found a reason to oppose Jesus and his inept disciples. The disciples failed to trust the promises Jesus had made earlier when he had sent them out to preach and heal (Matthew 10). They argued helplessly instead of praying and trusting in the Lord's power.

The people in the crowd were taking sides. When Jesus arrived, perhaps they were more curious about whether he would heal than about the message he proclaimed. The father was interested in solving his son's physical ailment, not in healing his own empty soul or the soul of his son. "O faithless generation," Jesus said. How far away from the glorious transfiguration this was!

But even with the crowd and all the chaos, Jesus found a way to not only show compassion but also teach a lesson. The father asked, "If you can do anything, have compassion on us and help us." Jesus said, "'If you can'! All things are possible for one who believes." Then the father realized his weakness: "I believe; help my unbelief!"

Jesus had never promised to heal everyone's diseases or solve everyone's troubles, but he was the glorious Son of God whom Peter, James, and John had seen on the mountaintop. Trusting and believing in Jesus did not ensure healing, but it did ensure God's love and help no matter the difficulty. Centering their faith in Jesus brought forgiveness, life, and salvation in the midst of chaos like that surrounding them here. Jesus invited this man to center his faith on the one the Father had sent—the Christ. In addition, Jesus healed the man's son.

And then a lesson for the disciples. After they left the father and son to rebuild their lives and the crowd to return to their homes, Jesus and the disciples went inside a house. The disciples' question was a natural one: "Why could we not cast it out?" We? The weakness of their thinking is clear in their question. Had they forgotten where the power came from? Had they depended so much on their own imagined power? No wonder they had failed. Jesus invited them to focus on the source of their power: prayer! He directed them to turn their attention to the source of all things and ask. He invited them to recognize that they were dependent upon a power from above that he had freely given them. Pray for that power in all situations.

PRAYER: Lord, life is not a mountaintop experience where I can look down on all the troubles of the world. Instead, I so often find myself in a messy, chaotic, and difficult place. When I do, draw my attention to you. Help me trust in you and not in my own power, intelligence, or wisdom. I will fail if I depend on myself. Center my heart, mind, and faith on your grace and love for me no matter what the troubles may be. Amen.

29

Betrayal?

[Jesus and his disciples] went on from there and passed through Galilee. And he did not want anyone to know, for he was teaching his disciples, saying to them, "The Son of Man is going to be delivered into the hands of men, and they will kill him. And when he is killed, after three days he will rise." But they did not understand the saying, and were afraid to ask him. (Mark 9:30-32)

Hiding. That word carries such a bad implication. Was Jesus hiding? He had traveled to Decapolis and Caesarea Philippi to avoid his Jewish critics. His movements were calculated so they did not draw attention to his presence and he could have some quiet time to teach his disciples. The crowds appeared from time to time like they did in Caesarea, but not like they had a year earlier in Galilee.

About the teaching moment in today's devotion Matthew says that the disciples came together in Galilee (Matthew 17:22). Did Jesus dismiss his disciples and send them on their own for a time? Did he give them instructions to meet together at some place in Galilee just as the angels announced in the empty tomb after he rose (Mark 16:7; Matthew 28:7)? Was it a little break? A rest? We don't know. But we do know that whatever happened, they came together in Galilee so Jesus could teach them.

Jesus repeated the grim announcement that he would be killed and then rise again. The first time the disciples heard this lesson was just before the transfiguration (Matthew 16:21-22; Mark 8:31-33; Luke 9:21-22). All the gospel writers except John mention that lesson. Matthew and Mark note Peter's rebuke of Jesus and the Savior's response.

That first announcement was a shock. Peter's reaction was understandable. The disciples had followed Jesus, loved him, and were dedicated to him and his teaching. But they did not understand the full details of his mission. They understood what Jesus had said in Nazareth at the synagogue (Luke 4:15-21), when he used the reading from Isaiah to reveal the first part of his mission: "The Spirit of the Lord is upon me, because he has anointed me to proclaim good news to the poor. He has sent me to proclaim liberty to the captives and recovering of sight to the blind, to set at liberty those who are oppressed, to proclaim the year of the Lord's favor" (Luke 4:18-19). They had seen and heard that mission carried out during the years of popularity in Galilee. Crowds had massed to hear him, and miracles had followed in the wake of his preaching and teaching. They were convinced that Jesus had the words of eternal life (John 6:68).

And in Caesarea, Jesus had revealed another important part of his mission—the most important part. He would suffer many things, be rejected, killed, and rise again after three days. The disciples could not imagine the opposition of the chief priests and teachers of the law growing to that point. Peter's rebuke of Jesus came from amazement at an idea he could not grasp. But Jesus was resolute and rebuked his ardent disciple. Perhaps the lesson slipped their memories, especially the memories of Peter, James, and John, who had seen the glory of the transfiguration. Jesus had told the three not to tell the others until he had risen from the dead. They had discussed what he meant by that but kept the glory on the mountain to themselves.

Now in Galilee but away from the crowds, Jesus repeated the lesson. There was no mistake about what they had heard in Caesarea. Jesus was telling them that others would kill him, but three days after his death he would rise again. This part of his ministry would happen as surely as his preaching and miracles had happened and continued to happen.

This time the prediction Jesus shared carried one disturbing idea the first one did not. Jesus said he would be "delivered into the hands of men." Betrayed! It was one thing to think that the Jerusalem critics would strengthen the plot to kill Jesus and then succeed. It was quite another to think he would be betrayed or handed over by someone who knew him. Who? Not only did they not understand, but they also were afraid to ask about it. Matthew tells us that the disciples were filled with grief.

Jesus clearly knew what was going to happen. He wanted to share enough of the future with his disciples so they would later understand. And they did. The word Jesus used to describe the betrayal would reappear in Matthew's gospel when Judas secretly arranged to hand Jesus over to the Jerusalem opposition (Matthew 26:15). But the identity of the betrayer remained hidden, even in the upper room, until the Garden of Gethsemane when Jesus asked Judas, using the same word, "Judas, would you betray the Son of Man with a kiss?" (Luke 22:48).

At this time, the sacrificial part of the Lord's mission was hidden from the disciples. That was evident when Peter took his sword to defend Jesus and the others ran away into the night. They hid on Saturday for fear of the Jews and even on Sunday night after they had heard the story of Jesus' resurrection. This part of his mission was the most important, and it was the heart of the message Peter and the others boldly proclaimed on Pentecost. Jesus suffered for the sins of the world. His blood, as John wrote, cleanses us from our sins (1 John 1:7)—not only our sins but also the sins of the whole world. That message would be the center of the disciples' work, the gospel they would sow into the field of the world as Jesus had directed (2 Corinthians 5:18-21). They had so much to learn yet.

PRAYER: Lord Jesus, you have paid the penalty for my sins and the sins of all the world when you were betrayed, killed, and rose again. So often I become distracted by my daily struggles and triumphs that I neglect the most important part of your mission. I even forget that on my own I am a lost and condemned creature, and I dismiss the message of your love and forgiveness. Teach me again and again that you came to cleanse me by your blood so that I may be declared righteous, holy, and your child and friend. Amen.

30

The Temple Tax

When they came to Capernaum, the collectors of the two-drachma tax went up to Peter and said, "Does your teacher not pay the tax?" He said, "Yes." And when he came into the house, Jesus spoke to him first, saying, "What do you think, Simon? From whom do kings of the earth take toll or tax? From their sons or from others?" And when he said, "From others," Jesus said to him, "Then the sons are free. However, not to give offense to them, go to the sea and cast a hook and take the first fish that comes up, and when you open its mouth you will find a shekel. Take that and give it to them for me and for yourself." (Matthew 17:24-27)

Jesus and his disciples made their way to Capernaum, the hub of Jesus' ministry a year earlier and the town where Peter, Andrew, James, and John had their fishing business. It was probably March or April because the temple tax was usually collected in March. But the tax collectors may not have been able to collect from Peter and the others because they were away from Capernaum for some time.

Peter was outside, perhaps at the seaside, and the others were inside when he was questioned about the tax. He hadn't paid his tax yet, but the tax collectors were more concerned whether Jesus had paid the tax. Perhaps they were looking for a way to discredit him and his ministry. After all, the tax was for the support of the temple and its ministry in Jerusalem, and every male was obligated to pay it whether he lived in Jerusalem or somewhere else. The tax amounted to about two days' wages. Peter assured them that Jesus had certainly paid the tax.

When Peter joined the others inside, Jesus asked Peter a question: "What do you think, Simon? From whom do kings of the earth take toll or tax? From their sons or from others?" The broader question put Peter's confession in Caesarea into a practical situation. Peter had said that Jesus was the Son of the living God, the Christ. Now Peter responded to Jesus by citing the principle that only ordinary subjects of the realm pay taxes. Sons of the king do not.

Under Peter's roof, where they were gathered, sat the King of kings, the Son of God. Should he pay the temple tax, or any tax for that matter? The principle was clear. He owed no taxes since sons of the king are exempt. We might extend the principle to include all children of God—the disciples and all believers. They were the adopted children of God, brothers and sisters of Jesus by faith. But it wasn't as simple as it seemed.

There was another issue. Jesus said, "Not to give offense to them." Failure to pay the tax would create an issue that could make it difficult for Jesus and his disciples to sow the seed of the gospel. Jesus had reminded them earlier that the kingdom of God meant sowing the seed of the gospel (Matthew 13). But that important work could be frustrated by asserting the exceptional position of Jesus. Paying the tax paved the way for the proclamation of the gospel. Refusing to pay the tax would cause an offense and therefore was an unnecessary hindrance to the gospel.

Jesus asserted his position as the Son of God and gave Peter a miraculous catch to pay the tax for himself and Peter. At the same time, he was showing the disciples that there would be times when they should not make an issue over matters that would cause offense and threaten to turn someone away from the gospel. Living in the world is not always black and white. There would be times when the brothers and sisters of Jesus would have to assert firmly God's truth. But there would also be times when they should be sensitive to others. When Jesus had told them he was sending them out like sheep among wolves, he also had told them to be "wise as serpents and innocent as doves" (Matthew 10:16).

In the next few months, Jesus would teach his disciples some practical truths for their work with others. They would travel to Jerusalem for the Feast of Booths, where Jesus would take an aggressive stand on his identity and the judgment to come on those who refused to believe. Matthew, Mark, and Luke record the practical lessons of the summer.

John's gospel tells us what happened at the Feast of Booths at the end of September and the Feast of the Dedication in December. From those days in Jerusalem, we have some of the most comforting words Jesus spoke and some of the clearest words about his identity.

PRAYER: Dear Lord Jesus, the Holy Spirit has called me through the gospel to be a believer—a child of God. I have the privilege of the blessings of my relationship with you—forgiveness, life, and salvation. I also have the noble task of sharing your gospel with others. Help me focus on the one thing that is important. Give me courage and strength to proclaim that gospel. Grant me wisdom to speak your truth with kindness and respect for others. Prevent me from creating unnecessary barriers that may cause offense and create barriers to your message. For your sake I pray. Amen.

31

The Greatest

> *An argument arose among them as to which of them was the greatest. But Jesus, knowing the reasoning of their hearts, took a child and put him by his side and said to them, "Whoever receives this child in my name receives me, and whoever receives me receives him who sent me. For he who is least among you all is the one who is great."* (Luke 9:46-48)

Still in Galilee, the disciples had a difficult lesson to learn. The lesson would need to be repeated. That necessity reveals what still troubles disciples of Jesus today. Disciples are forgiven and have eternal life by faith in their Savior, but they do not lose the sinful nature. It hangs on to us tenaciously to battle against the new self that desires to serve Jesus and others.

Who is the greatest? The discussion among the disciples erupted into an argument. Had they created a hierarchy that came from their first missionary journey? Jesus had sent out the Twelve to the lost sheep of Israel with the message he had proclaimed from the beginning: "The kingdom of heaven is at hand" (Matthew 10:7). He also had given them the power to heal and drive out demons with the encouragement, "You received without paying; give without pay" (Matthew 10:8). When they returned to Jesus, they related and compared their experiences. Did some of those stories reveal that some had more success than others? Did they compare their trophies?

Perhaps the discussion grew out of the choice of Peter, James, and John in Caesarea at the transfiguration of Jesus. They had gone up the mountainside and were told not to tell what they had seen while the others remained below. On another occasion, Peter had taken the lead in answering who they thought Jesus was, and Jesus had called Peter the rock. Were the disciples looking for telltale signs that implied a favorite of Jesus? What about the disciple described as the one Jesus loved and who ended up next to him in the upper room (John 13:23)? They knew their discussion was wrong and tried to keep it from Jesus.

But Jesus knew. Perhaps they disguised their discussion with a question about greatness. Matthew records that they asked, "Who is the greatest in the kingdom of heaven?" (18:1). But Jesus knows the human heart and its quest for superiority. That quest was true even among the disciples. Jesus' approach provided a vivid lesson that stayed with them even if the lesson on humble service had to be repeated. He took a little child standing next to him as an object lesson. I can easily imagine Jesus drawing the child close and putting his hand on the child's shoulder or head. Perhaps other children were present too, all curious about Jesus. The embarrassed disciples gave Jesus their undivided attention.

Jesus gave two profound answers to the question of who was the greatest. The first is a lesson in humbly serving others—including little children: "Whoever receives this child in my name receives me, and whoever receives me receives him who sent me." Important people who are noted for their accomplishments or prestige are not the greatest. Nor is greatness measured by a person's association with important and influential people. We may do these things to show how great we are or how important we want to be. But greatness is seeing others—no matter their stature in the world—and treating them with respect and warmth, welcoming them. The child at Jesus' side was the lesson.

How different that was from the disciples' contentious struggle over who was the greatest. What Jesus was teaching ran counter to all they knew and saw in the world around them. The world was always seeking to crown someone as the greatest. But Jesus had come to change them. He gave them new birth—a new self within—that turns away from a drive for superiority and toward love for others. He desired his disciples to change on the inside—to see others as opportunities to love, help, and befriend.

Something else to remember: The disciples were to see others as if they wore the face of Jesus. Whoever welcomes them welcomes me, Jesus said, and whoever welcomes me welcomes God above. Their goal as believers in Jesus was to welcome others with a humble and sincere spirit. They were not to argue about who is better or who did more. They were to welcome others—love them—and in that process they would show others Jesus and his heavenly Father. Jesus had shown such love in his miracles, and he would show it in the months ahead. Perhaps John was thinking about what Jesus was teaching here when he wrote, "Beloved, let us love one another, for love is from God, and whoever loves has been born of God and knows God. In this is love, not that we have loved God but that he loved us and sent his Son to be the propitiation for our sins" (1 John 4:7,10).

PRAYER: Lord Jesus, you love me. I do not deserve such love. Your love has changed me to love others. Unfortunately, the desire to be great and superior to others is a powerful force that continues to pull me away from my desire to love others humbly. Forgive me, Lord. Help me find in your undeserved love for me a desire to reflect that love. Help me see your face in those around me so that I might show them respect and love. From one who so easily abandons love for others, I pray for strength to love as you have loved me. Amen.

32

Not One Should Perish

"Whoever causes one of these little ones who believe in me to sin, it would be better for him to have a great millstone fastened around his neck and to be drowned in the depth of the sea. Woe to the world for temptations to sin! For it is necessary that temptations come, but woe to the one by whom the temptation comes! And if your hand or your foot causes you to sin, cut it off and throw it away. It is better for you to enter life crippled or lame than with two hands or two feet to be thrown into the eternal fire. And if your eye causes you to sin, tear it out and throw it away. It is better for you to enter life with one eye than with two eyes to be thrown into the hell of fire. See that you do not despise one of these little ones. For I tell you that in heaven their angels always see the face of my Father who is in heaven. What do you think? If a man has a hundred sheep, and one of them has gone astray, does he not leave the ninety-nine on the mountains and go in search of the one that went astray? And if he finds it, truly, I say to you, he rejoices over it more than over the ninety-nine that never went astray. So it is not the will of my Father who is in heaven that one of these little ones should perish." (Matthew 18:6-14)

The child at Jesus' side had been an unforgettable object lesson. The one who is the greatest is not who the world thinks is the greatest. Instead, the one who loves quietly and without fanfare is the greatest. That great one understands that he or she serves Jesus himself when treating others, including children, with kindness, gentleness, and love.

But Jesus had more to say. He explained *why* it was important for his disciples to love humbly and be concerned about others. Jesus began with a graphic warning for those who cause little ones—"these . . . who believe in me"—to stumble. Certainly, he had children in mind, but all people are included in his warning, "Woe to the world for temptations to sin!" This warning is much broader than little children.

The warning is not vague and indefinite. For someone who causes believers to stumble, "it would be better for him to have a great millstone fastened around his neck and to be drowned in the depth of the sea." Such a fate means the offender is obliterated from memory, forgotten in the depths of the sea.

Jesus was reminding his disciples what they already knew. The world is full of things that cause believers to stumble. The disciples would stumble: Peter with his pride as he stepped toward the warmth of the fire in the high priest's courtyard. All of them running away because of fear in the garden. And certainly Judas, whose hands reached for betrayal money. The opposition they had faced and would continue to face caused them trouble, doubts, and confusion.

There would always be things that cause people to stumble, but the disciples of Jesus should not be the cause. Their lives, their words, and their teaching should leave no doubt about how important the faith of others ought to be. That's the why. We must be careful not to cause a believer to stumble and lose his or her faith because of us and something we did. Woe to the world because of those things that cause believers to stumble. Woe especially to the person through whom they come.

Jesus also looked at the personal side of a believer's walk of faith. Stumbling can also be personal. Jesus suggested drastic action for individual believers to take lest they stumble, lose faith, and therefore are "thrown into the eternal fire." To go through life without a foot or a hand or eyes is better than being thrown into the fire of hell and barred from entering eternal life. The reason is clear: Life in heaven is more important than anything else we may experience here, including the unhindered power to see, walk, and touch.

And there is more. The Father in heaven—our Father in heaven—watches over his believers. He sends his angels to do his bidding for the benefit of the "little ones," which includes all believers of all sizes and ages. If God shows such interest in his own, we should not be careless and cause anyone to stumble. We should also keep watch that we do not stumble ourselves.

Our heavenly Father wants nothing to keep people from eternal life. This lesson of Jesus was for the disciples and for us also. So easily do we stumble, and so easily we cause others to stumble and fall away. Keep yourself and others on the narrow path to life. Do not cause anyone to stumble and wander off that path.

Believers should be concerned about those around them—not only about their health and welfare but also about their spiritual relationship to Jesus. As he talked with his disciples here, he emphasized this by telling the parable of the wandering sheep, which concludes with this point: "It is not the will of my Father who is in heaven that one of these little ones should perish."

Jesus was the expression of that will of the Father. He came into this world to seek and save the lost, to suffer for the sins of the world and bring eternal life for all. The people of the world were at the heart of his mission. His message to the people of the world is a call to repent—to turn away from their wandering ways and turn to him to feel his warm, welcome embrace.

The lesson was for the disciples of all time. We are to go and make disciples. The work of Jesus and the work of his disciples over centuries is part of the one important principle of God, who is not willing "that one of these little ones should perish."

PRAYER: Lord Jesus, you have found me and called me to accept the promises you made to all people. Keep me from wandering away from the path of life. Help me never to cause anyone else to wander away from your promises by my behavior or words. May I prize your promises above all else so that I may enter your courts when this life is over. Amen.

33

Forgiven, Therefore Forgive

Then Peter came up and said to [Jesus], "Lord, how often will my brother sin against me, and I forgive him? As many as seven times?" Jesus said to him, "I do not say to you seven times, but seventy-seven times. Therefore the kingdom of heaven may be compared to a king who wished to settle accounts with his servants. When he began to settle, one was brought to him who owed him ten thousand talents. And since he could not pay, his master ordered him to be sold, with his wife and children and all that he had, and payment to be made. So the servant fell on his knees, imploring him, 'Have patience with me, and I will pay you everything.' And out of pity for him, the master of that servant released him and forgave him the debt. But when that same servant went out, he found one of his fellow servants who owed him a hundred denarii, and seizing him, he began to choke him, saying, 'Pay what you owe.' So his fellow servant fell down and pleaded with him, 'Have patience with me, and I will pay you.' He refused and went and put him in prison until he should pay the debt. When his fellow servants saw what had taken place, they were greatly distressed, and they went and reported to their master all that had taken place. Then his master summoned him and said to him, 'You wicked servant! I forgave you all that debt because you pleaded with me. And should not you have had mercy on your fellow servant, as I had mercy on you?' And in anger his master delivered him to the jailers, until he should pay all his debt. So also my heavenly Father will do to every one of you, if you do not forgive your brother from your heart." (Matthew 18:21-35)

These lessons from Jesus stretched into everyday life. Peter did not ask a deep theological question or engage in a theoretical issue that required deep intellectual concepts. It was a practical question about forgiveness. "How often will my brother sin against me, and I forgive him?" He had an imagined limit in his mind—seven times—and it recognized two things. First, as Christians live in this world, they will injure, lie to, or take advantage of others. One will speak ill of even the good intentions of another. Situations will develop that require one brother or sister to forgive another.

The second practical issue is that brothers and sisters do not wish to be taken advantage of and forgive the same person guilty of the same offense again and again. They long to see some improvement in the behavior of others they have forgiven. What should Peter do? How long should he put up with being hurt? When should he stop forgiving?

These questions still exist in the minds of believers even though we live centuries later and our world is so different. We still have such questions because we are hurt by the words and actions of others. Even among believers, one may injure another. Marriages and families suffer from the pain of angry words and thoughtless actions—sometimes even deliberate and calculated actions intended to cause pain. We still have the sinful nature that always has difficulty with doing what the Lord wants. Maintaining a kind, forgiving, compassionate, and loving attitude toward others when we feel wronged or when others take advantage of us can be very difficult. We can repeat Peter's question. What do we do?

Jesus answered, "The kingdom of heaven may be compared to . . ." and told the parable of the unmerciful servant. In this parable was one who graciously and freely forgave the debt of his servant. The servant's debt was too large to repay—10,000 bags of gold. "Bags of gold" is a translation for "talent"—20 years of wages. The debt was enormous. The consequence of this debt was debtors' prison, not just for him but for his entire family.

Faced with such a debt, the servant pleaded for mercy. It was his only hope. If he had enough time, he hoped to repay everything. Both he and the king were well aware that the task could never be done, but the king took pity on him and cancelled the debt.

The parable teaches an important lesson for Peter and for us. The indebted servant was free of the huge debt, but he could not find it in his heart to forgive another servant whose debt was paltry by comparison (one day's wages). He clearly had not been moved by the king's gracious forgiveness of his great debt. Although the servant had escaped prison, when he heard his fellow servant's cry for mercy, he put the other servant in prison. This man reveals himself as a "wicked servant" because he learned nothing from the king's forgiveness. He remained wicked and unmoved.

Is there is any doubt about the point? Jesus clarifies, "So also my heavenly Father will do to every one of you, if you do not forgive your brother from your heart." How often should we forgive others? That question disappears in the lesson. Peter learns that in the kingdom of heaven, forgiveness is a way of thinking and a way of acting. God forgives. We should be changed by our heavenly Father's gracious forgiveness so that we forgive others. The debt we owe is more than we can ever repay, but God forgives. What others do to us when they speak badly of us or even deliberately seek to injure us or cause us trouble is a paltry debt by comparison. Our hearts are not to remain "wicked." Instead, they are to be motivated by the forgiveness of our heavenly Father so that we can forgive our fellow servants. A lesson for all times, but a lesson not easy to practice.

PRAYER: Heavenly Father, you have forgiven me for the great debt I owe to you. I am unable to do enough even if you give me eternity to right every wrong and make up for every infraction of your commandments. Yet you forgive me. Jesus has paid for all my sins, and you declare me free of the consequences of my many sins. May your gracious forgiveness work in my heart an attitude of forgiveness to others. When I wish to withhold forgiveness for the injury others have inflicted on me, open my eyes to see the great forgiveness you have given me so that I can forgive. Amen.

34

Going to Judea

After this Jesus went about in Galilee. He would not go about in Judea, because the Jews were seeking to kill him. Now the Jews' Feast of Booths was at hand. So his brothers said to him, "Leave here and go to Judea, that your disciples also may see the works you are doing. For no one works in secret if he seeks to be known openly. If you do these things, show yourself to the world." For not even his brothers believed in him. Jesus said to them, "My time has not yet come, but your time is always here. The world cannot hate you, but it hates me because I testify about it that its works are evil. You go up to the feast. I am not going up to this feast, for my time has not yet fully come." After saying this, he remained in Galilee. But after his brothers had gone up to the feast, then he also went up, not publicly but in private. The Jews were looking for him at the feast, and saying, "Where is he?" And there was much muttering about him among the people. While some said, "He is a good man," others said, "No, he is leading the people astray." Yet for fear of the Jews no one spoke openly of him. (John 7:1-13)

It was late September or early October. The harvest was done! The Feast of Booths was at hand. For faithful Jews that meant a thanksgiving celebration and a trip to Jerusalem. Through Moses, God had directed his people to celebrate the Feast of Booths on the 15th day of the seventh month "when you have gathered in the produce of the land" (Leviticus 23:39). The festival started five days after the Day of Atonement (Leviticus 23:26-32) and lasted seven days, with a sacred assembly on the first and last days. God intended it to be a "statute forever throughout your generations" (Leviticus 23:41).

The festival was sometimes referred to as the "in-gathering" because of the harvest, but God gave it a better name, the Feast of Booths, because of the unique regulation God had commanded: "You shall dwell in booths for seven days" (Leviticus 23:42). People were to abandon their homes in order to live in booths for the weeklong festival.

This annual celebration was more than a thanksgiving celebration or harvest festival. The booths were a reminder that the Israelites had lived in temporary shelters when the Lord brought them out of Egypt. Of course, the Passover celebrated the deliverance from Egypt. Once they had left Egypt behind, they faced the harsh sun of the wilderness and lived in temporary shelters.

It was a strange and different life for the Israelites. Water and food were scarce while sunshine and heat were abundant. God brought them out of Egypt and graciously took care of their needs. First, he provided manna, or bread, every day except the Sabbath. Then he also provided water for the people, sometimes bringing water out of a rock. Finally, the Lord led them through the wilderness with a pillar of fire by night and a pillar of cloud by day to assure them that he was always with them.

John tells us about Jesus at the Feast of Booths in the last year of Jesus' ministry. The festival brought Jesus and his disciples to Jerusalem about six months before the Passover when Jesus was crucified. In the years before this festival, Jesus and his disciples had sown the seed of the gospel in Galilee and other places. Some of those seeds had sprouted, while others had not sprouted or grown to maturity.

It was time to travel to Jerusalem. Jesus' family, specifically his brothers (perhaps cousins), encouraged him to go to Jerusalem, but not for the harvest festival celebration or to thank God for his care of his people in the wilderness or even for his continual care of them every day. They wanted Jesus to gain a reputation for himself in Jerusalem. They advised Jesus, "Leave here and go to Judea. . . . No one works in secret if he seeks to be known openly. . . . Show yourself to the world." They may have had more on their minds than just encouraging Jesus to gain popularity in Judea. Perhaps they also hoped to bask in the limelight of their famous relative.

But Jesus had his mission clearly in mind. In the past few months he had avoided Jerusalem and Judea in order to teach his disciples quietly, away from the criticism and controversy that would have arisen there. Jesus saw clearly what lay ahead at the next Passover. He had been telling his disciples what would happen even though they did not understand. Now he said, "My time has not yet come." This time he would not enter Jerusalem to the shouts of acclamation and welcome. That would come, but not now. God had given the command that faithful and devout Jews should go to Jerusalem. Jesus would be obedient and go. But he entered Jerusalem quietly. Once he and his disciples arrived, they probably purchased or found branches to build their *sukkahs,* or booths. But they did not go with his family.

Jesus knew well what he would experience in Jerusalem. As the festival began, the Jewish leaders were looking for him. He appeared without notice, just a simple Jewish pilgrim living like everyone else in a temporary shelter. Curiosity and speculation ran through the crowds. People's opinions about Jesus included those who thought he was a good man and others who thought he was a deceiver. For now he was just a curiosity for most. But he was much more than that to the Jewish leaders. They were looking for an opportunity to discredit him once and for all. If they knew he was in Jerusalem, they would attack him and even try to kill him. Yet Jesus left Jerusalem unscathed this time. His time had not yet come.

PRAYER: Jesus, you are the Christ, true God come to earth. You became flesh and made your temporary home with us. I praise and thank you for all the blessings you give to me and all people. Like the birds, you feed us and give us protection. Yet you have also taught us that this life is only temporary, like the booths used for the Feast of Booths. You came to give us a permanent home with you in heaven. May my gratitude for all I have in this life be mixed with the realization that it is only a temporary home that will disappear when I stand before you in glory. Amen.

35

Teaching From God Above

About the middle of the feast Jesus went up into the temple and began teaching. The Jews therefore marveled, saying, "How is it that this man has learning, when he has never studied?" So Jesus answered them, "My teaching is not mine, but his who sent me. If anyone's will is to do God's will, he will know whether the teaching is from God or whether I am speaking on my own authority. The one who speaks on his own authority seeks his own glory; but the one who seeks the glory of him who sent him is true, and in him there is no falsehood. Has not Moses given you the law? Yet none of you keeps the law. Why do you seek to kill me?" The crowd answered, "You have a demon! Who is seeking to kill you?" Jesus answered them, "I did one work, and you all marvel at it. Moses gave you circumcision (not that it is from Moses, but from the fathers), and you circumcise a man on the Sabbath. If on the Sabbath a man receives circumcision, so that the law of Moses may not be broken, are you angry with me because on the Sabbath I made a man's whole body well? Do not judge by appearances, but judge with right judgment." (John 7:14-24)

Among the thousands of booths in Jerusalem during the Feast of Booths, one of them housed Jesus. Perhaps a cluster of them surrounded the one Jesus used. They may have been filled with the faithful who came with him. So many booths! The streets and the places outside the walls were filled with them. Imagine a large campsite filled with thousands of booths and the booth of Jesus somewhere among them. He had come quietly to obey the command to attend and give thanks.

Halfway through the festival, he left his booth and went to the temple to teach. Whatever he said stirred those who heard him. They were amazed and wondered how he could speak such truth without an education. A dialogue began that would continue through the remaining days of the festival. The themes of this dialogue were important to anyone even remotely interested in who Jesus was. John was present, and no doubt so were the other disciples. They are not mentioned, but John recorded what happened and gave special prominence to the words of Jesus and his critics.

When Jesus noticed the amazement of the Jews, he responded with a provocative defense of his teaching: "My teaching is not mine, but his who sent me." He made it clear that he had not come to gain personal glory with his teaching. He had a different motive than what even his own relatives thought. His brothers urged him to go to Jerusalem and show himself to the world (John 7:3-5). His motive was to share with those who were attending the festival a teaching that came from God and to give God glory.

Anyone can claim that the message is from God. Who can prove that what is said comes from God or from someone's own imagination or intelligence? That question had been raised by the critics of Jesus and is still raised in our own age. The disciples could testify that Jesus was telling the truth. Matthew could and did cite the Old Testament prophecies Jesus fulfilled. All of the disciples could serve as eyewitnesses to his miracles. In our own age, those miracles tend to be categorized as myths, illusions, or just fabrications of wishful thinking. The crowd at Jesus' baptism heard the voice from heaven identify the source of Jesus' words and power. Peter, James, and John stood with Jesus, Moses, and Elijah and heard the voice from heaven also direct them to "listen to him" (Matthew 17:5; Mark 9:7; Luke 9:35). Here the disciples were silent because that was what Jesus had asked of them. They would speak, but only after he rose from the dead, which was another demonstration of the source of his teaching.

Jesus understood the criticism and the depth of those who opposed him. He asked, "Why do you seek to kill me?" That was, of course, part of his mission—to die for the sins of the world. He had told his disciples it would happen, but this was not the time for it to happen. The death of Jesus was a reality sought by the religious leaders of the Jews, but they were seeking to silence him, not to save the world.

Those who had come to the festival knew that the leaders opposed Jesus, so they kept their conversations about Jesus private "for fear of the Jews" (John 7:13).

To make this threat public would be a bold and aggressive step because the secret plot would lose its cover. So the Jewish opposition took another approach: character assassination and bluster. They hid their opposition and refusal to accept the words of Jesus, accusing him, "You have a demon!" It was a familiar tactic, but Jesus met it head-on by citing a miracle he had performed in Jerusalem.

Earlier in the year, perhaps at the Passover or at the Pentecost festival, Jesus had come to Jerusalem for the "feast of the Jews" (John 5:1). He healed a man on the Sabbath, telling him to take his mat and walk. He showed compassion and concern on the Sabbath but was criticized for telling the man to do what was contrary to the Sabbath laws: carry his mat. Jesus reminded the crowd that they also broke the Sabbath laws whenever they performed a circumcision on the Sabbath. That revealed their double standard. It was all right for them to work on the Sabbath and circumcise, but it was not all right for Jesus to heal. Jesus had concluded, "Do not judge by appearances, but judge with right judgment."

The conversation would continue during the festival and continues down to our age. Does Jesus speak the truth or does he not? Look through the record left by the eyewitnesses and "judge with right judgment."

PRAYER: Jesus, you came from heaven to dwell with us and teach us. Many people today think you had great thoughts and profound words that flowed from your own thinking and intelligence. When I hear their criticism, help me do what your heavenly Father told the disciples to do: "Listen." Even when I have questions and doubts about the Scriptures, help me trust them because they are the words of God. Amen.

36

When the Messiah Comes

Some of the people of Jerusalem therefore said, "Is not this the man whom they seek to kill? And here he is, speaking openly, and they say nothing to him! Can it be that the authorities really know that this is the Christ? But we know where this man comes from, and when the Christ appears, no one will know where he comes from." So Jesus proclaimed, as he taught in the temple, "You know me, and you know where I come from. But I have not come of my own accord. He who sent me is true, and him you do not know. I know him, for I come from him, and he sent me." So they were seeking to arrest him, but no one laid a hand on him, because his hour had not yet come. Yet many of the people believed in him. They said, "When the Christ appears, will he do more signs than this man has done?" The Pharisees heard the crowd muttering these things about him, and the chief priests and Pharisees sent officers to arrest him. Jesus then said, "I will be with you a little longer, and then I am going to him who sent me. You will seek me and you will not find me. Where I am you cannot come." The Jews said to one another, "Where does this man intend to go that we will not find him? Does he intend to go to the Dispersion among the Greeks and teach the Greeks? What does he mean by saying, 'You will seek me and you will not find me,' and, 'Where I am you cannot come'?" (John 7:25-36)

Jesus had asked the disciples in Caesarea, "Who do people say that the Son of Man is?" (Matthew 16:13). Peter had quickly said, "You are the Christ, the Son of the living God" (Matthew 16:16). For many here in Jerusalem, the answer was not as clear. Their conversations about Jesus were private because they were afraid of their leaders who were looking for Jesus. Jesus had even asked the crowd, "Why do you seek to kill me?" (John 7:19). Now they wondered if he was the Messiah. Jesus was teaching publicly and unchallenged in the temple. After listening to him, could the Jewish leaders have concluded that he was the Messiah?

The people were confused about Jesus. They were confused about what the Scriptures said about his origin and what he would come to accomplish. Did they understand the words of Daniel that the Messiah would suddenly appear with no indication of where he came from? "I saw in the night visions, and behold, with the clouds of heaven there came one like a son of man" (Daniel 7:13). Did they remember Malachi's prophecy? "The Lord whom you seek will suddenly come to his temple; and the messenger of the covenant in whom you delight, behold, he is coming, says the LORD of hosts" (Malachi 3:1).

They knew Jesus as the carpenter from Galilee. No doubt many of them had been in the crowds of Galilee or at least had heard of his ministry there. How could this be the Messiah? The people of Nazareth had raised the same objection when Jesus had identified himself as the fulfillment of Isaiah's prophecy. They knew his brothers and his family and asked, "Is not this Joseph's son?" (Luke 4:22). The people of Nazareth had been ready to kill him then, but it was not time yet.

But suddenly as Jesus was teaching in the temple, he knew what the people were saying about him and responded by crying out what he had said before: "You know me, and you know where I come from. But I have not come of my own accord. He who sent me is true." Jesus was the Messiah sent from heaven. He spoke for God above. He was the messenger of the covenant with the truth for all humanity. The people were confused about him, but not because they misunderstood the passages. Like those in Nazareth, they could not accept that he was the fulfillment of all the prophecies of the coming Messiah. Jesus brutally denounces their unbelief: "Him you do not know." That is, the one who had sent him, the God of Abraham, Isaac, and Jacob.

Those words pushed the people beyond merely challenging words. It drove them to rage and a desire to seize him and silence what they considered blasphemy. They rejected Jesus. But as in Nazareth, they could not touch him. His hour had not yet come. But not all in the crowd rejected him. Many wondered if this teacher in the temple during the Feast of Booths was indeed the Messiah. The Pharisees wanted to stop anyone from entertaining that idea. So they sent the temple guards to arrest Jesus.

Jesus gave the people one more warning: "I will be with you a little longer, and then I am going to him who sent me." Jesus had already told his disciples what was ahead—his betrayal, suffering, death, and resurrection. He had a mission to fulfill. Six months later it would be accomplished. He would ascend "to him who sent" Jesus. The disciples didn't fully grasp this yet, but Jesus was telling them and the people in the temple that his mission was not to bring world peace or victory over the Roman occupying armies or even a perfect world without trouble and pain. He knew his mission and what it was. God had sent him so that whoever believed in him would not perish but have everlasting life.

Some of these Jews would reject him. They would continue to look for a Messiah of their own understanding—one who would correct the oppression and evil of the world and make it perfect. But he had come to forgive sins and provide victory over death itself. They would keep looking for the wrong Messiah and not find the true Messiah who taught that day in their temple. They did not understand what he was saying and, because they had rejected the way there, could not go where he was going. They rejected him.

In the upper room a few months later, the disciples were confused too. Jesus had told them that he would go to prepare a place for them. They were confused about how they were to get there, but Jesus explained, "I am the way, and the truth, and the life. No one comes to the Father except through me" (John 14:6).

PRAYER: Jesus, you have sent the Holy Spirit so that I might believe in you. I believe that you are the Way, the Truth, and the Life. Keep me strong in my faith so I may treasure the blessings of forgiveness, life, and salvation that you have won for me. Preserve me in that faith so I do not seek another and look for other blessings. Amen.

37

Rivers of Living Water

On the last day of the feast, the great day, Jesus stood up and cried out, "If anyone thirsts, let him come to me and drink. Whoever believes in me, as the Scripture has said, 'Out of his heart will flow rivers of living water.'" Now this he said about the Spirit, whom those who believed in him were to receive, for as yet the Spirit had not been given, because Jesus was not yet glorified. When they heard these words, some of the people said, "This really is the Prophet." Others said, "This is the Christ." But some said, "Is the Christ to come from Galilee? Has not the Scripture said that the Christ comes from the offspring of David, and comes from Bethlehem, the village where David was?" So there was a division among the people over him. Some of them wanted to arrest him, but no one laid hands on him. (John 7:37-44)

The Feast of Booths began with a sacred assembly when no one should do regular work. It was a day of rest—a special Sabbath rest as God had commanded. God also had commanded the people to live in temporary shelters for seven days to commemorate how the Israelites lived when God brought them out of Egypt. The final day was also special: "On the eighth day you shall hold a holy convocation and present a food offering to the LORD. It is a solemn assembly; you shall not do any ordinary work" (Leviticus 23:36).

The entire festival was a joyous event of thanksgiving and praise to God for the harvest and for his care of the Israelites in the wilderness and every day since. Moses summarized the history of the Israelites in the wilderness in Deuteronomy: "Take care lest you forget the LORD your God . . . who led you through the great and terrifying wilderness, with its fiery serpents and scorpions and thirsty ground where there was no water, who brought you water out of the flinty rock, who fed you in the wilderness with manna that your fathers did not know, that he might humble you and test you, to do you good in the end" (Deuteronomy 8:11,15-16).

The temporary shelters of the people in Jerusalem during the festival week reminded them of the Israelites' journey. Water was an important feature of their wandering in the wilderness, but the regulations for the festival did not mention water as part of the festival. But after God's Old Testament people returned from their Babylonian captivity, they added a reminder of the rock and the water. A ceremony was introduced that included priests going to the pool of Siloam in order to bring water to the temple. On the last day of the festival, the priests poured out the water in a special ceremony at the altar.

Whether this ceremony was used when Jesus was in Jerusalem for this festival, we don't know. And we cannot be sure whether he chose to speak while the water was being poured out. Neither John nor any of the other writers confirm the event or the timing. But we do know that Jesus spoke about water. It was a dramatic announcement "on the last day of the feast, the great day." He boldly claimed that he was the source of water to quench the thirst of every human heart just as he had done with the Samaritan woman at the well in Samaria (John 4:1-15).

He had told the Samaritan woman at the well that he was the source of living water that would give eternal life (John 4:14). He claimed the power to give eternal life in many ways through his ministry. At the feeding of the five thousand, he also referred to the manna Moses gave the people in the wilderness and boldly proclaimed he was the Bread of Life from heaven who could give eternal life (John 6:35).

Jesus satisfies the deepest thirst of the human soul—a thirst for peace with God and for enduring love and forgiveness from God. Not only do those who drink and believe in him possess God's faithful love and its gift of eternal life, but his life-giving water also fills them so full that the living water flows from within their hearts to others. John was there. He heard what Jesus said and inserted a reminder that these words of Jesus were fulfilled later. The water of life would flow from the hearts and lips of the disciples on Pentecost when the Spirit brought thousands to believe in Jesus through their words. The water of life would then spread throughout the world as believers shared the gospel.

The dramatic announcement was an invitation to all who attended that final assembly. The loud words of Jesus echoed off the walls of the temple in Jerusalem, where his enemies lined the streets and sought to kill him. When he had said that God above had sent him, the Pharisees had sent the temple guards to seize him, and here "some of them wanted to arrest him." But it did not happen—not yet. His hour had not yet come.

Some in the crowd were convinced he was the Messiah and would take his teachings home with them. Jesus had sown the seed. After his resurrection, some of those seeds would mature and people would possess the living water that would flow from within them to quench the spiritual thirst of others.

Yet others still found a reason not to believe. This man was from Galilee and therefore couldn't be the Messiah. The Messiah had to come from Bethlehem. The chief priests and teachers of the law had directed the Magi to Bethlehem to worship the King of the Jews. They chose not to remember.

PRAYER: Lord Jesus, "I stretch out my hands to you; my soul thirsts for you like a parched land" (Psalm 143:6). You have filled my soul with living water and given me hope, comfort, and strength. May the water of life you have given me flow out of my heart like a river to others in my compassion for them, in my words of tender comfort, and whenever I share the truth of the living water of your grace. For your sake I ask for courage to speak even when confronted by opposition as you did in Jerusalem. Amen.

38

Behind Closed Doors

The officers then came to the chief priests and Pharisees, who said to them, "Why did you not bring him?" The officers answered, "No one ever spoke like this man!" The Pharisees answered them, "Have you also been deceived? Have any of the authorities or the Pharisees believed in him? But this crowd that does not know the law is accursed." Nicodemus, who had gone to him before, and who was one of them, said to them, "Does our law judge a man without first giving him a hearing and learning what he does?" They replied, "Are you from Galilee too? Search and see that no prophet arises from Galilee." (John 7:45-52)

We get a look behind the scenes near the end of the festival. Perhaps the crowds listening to Jesus were still in the courtyard. It was still the special Sabbath rest on the last day of the festival, but things were winding down. At sunset, another day would begin and the booths would be dismantled and discarded as families headed home.

But before the last day was over, the officers returned to the chief priests and Pharisees. The Jewish leaders had sent them to arrest Jesus, but they were prevented from completing their task. Once they found Jesus, he was likely surrounded by a large crowd. That made it difficult to get to him. As the officers waited for an opportunity, they listened. What they heard was more important than their orders to arrest this teacher. "No one ever spoke like this man!"

The leaders were not happy. Their opposition to Jesus was the reason they wanted him arrested. They had accused him of breaking the Sabbath regulations on more than one occasion. They had heard of his miracle on the Sabbath in Galilee (Matthew 12:1-14). Then Jesus had asserted that he was the Lord of the Sabbath. They had accused him of healing and casting out demons by the power of Beelzebul

(Matthew 12:22-37). He had even healed a man on the Sabbath in Jerusalem (John 5:1-9). And during the Feast of Booths, they had a running debate with Jesus about where he came from and who had given him the authority to say what he said.

Jesus had responded to all the charges and sent them away with no way to counter his arguments. But they had a response. They continued to criticize Jesus publicly and privately, hoping to discredit him and diminish his popularity. They considered him a threat to their positions as leaders of the Jewish nation. So after Jesus had silenced them, they concentrated on another strategy. They plotted to kill Jesus (John 5:18; Matthew 12:14). They sought to seize him more than once at the festival, and Jesus had asked, "Why do you seek to kill me?" (John 7:19). The guards were only one example of their hostility and opposition to Jesus.

The officers listened but did not hear threats, blasphemy, or a perversion of the Scriptures and the Sabbath regulations. Jesus had honored the Sabbath rest included in the festival commands of God. They were witnesses of that as well as the words of Jesus. But the Pharisees were locked in unalterable opposition to Jesus. For them it was a power struggle for their religious life as it had developed over the centuries. Jesus threatened to overturn it all and, in their thinking, had to be eliminated. About six months later, Caiaphas would advise that Jesus had to be sacrificed for the sake of the nation (John 11:50).

What to do with those who think differently? The officers offered a different perspective to the hard-line opposition to Jesus. What to do? The Pharisees did what opponents to the truth often do. They bullied those who thought differently: "Have you also been deceived?" No proof, but simply a portrait of Jesus as a deceiver. This is a characteristic strategy of a bully: belittle the opponent and call him or her names. But they were not done yet. "Have any of the authorities or the Pharisees believed in him?" They appealed to an acknowledged authority: the rulers and Pharisees. Everyone else, even the leaders, had rejected Jesus. "How can you still believe in him?" That too is a tactic of bullies.

The Pharisees' claim of superior intelligence and importance also comes with a little name-calling: "This crowd that does not know the law is accursed." That is, anyone who thinks differently must be wrong and stupid; they are cursed and can't see the truth. Sound familiar? The enemies of Jesus and the Scriptures haven't changed their characteristic attacks on believers down to the present.

One more example of their bullying comes when Nicodemus attempts to inject some common sense into the discussion. He quotes the law, "Does our law judge a man without first giving him a hearing and learning what he does?" It is a challenge to their rush to judgment—a common sense question based on a legal and religious principle. Nicodemus was not part of their condemnation of Jesus and wanted to return to principles. But it would not happen on this day! Again, the bullies belittled Nicodemus by calling him one of those backward and ignorant Galileans. Retaining the same tone of superiority, they cited Scripture and used it as a club: "Search and see that no prophet arises from Galilee."

But they were wrong, just as wrong as those who claimed that Jesus couldn't be the Messiah because he did not come from Bethlehem (John 7:42). The rulers and Pharisees neglected to see that Scripture does speak of Galilee. "In the former time he brought into contempt the land of Zebulun and the land of Naphtali, but in the latter time he has made glorious the way of the sea, the land beyond the Jordan, Galilee of the nations. The people who walked in darkness have seen a great light; those who dwelt in a land of deep darkness, on them has light shone" (Isaiah 9:1-2).

PRAYER: Lord Jesus, you have called me to be your disciple and given me the privilege of sharing your truth with those around me. When they oppose me and your message, give me strength to remain faithful. When they seek to intimidate me or bully me to abandon you, help me remain strong in my faith. For your sake. Amen.

39

Light of the World

Again Jesus spoke to them, saying, "I am the light of the world. Whoever follows me will not walk in darkness, but will have the light of life." So the Pharisees said to him, "You are bearing witness about yourself; your testimony is not true." Jesus answered, "Even if I do bear witness about myself, my testimony is true, for I know where I came from and where I am going, but you do not know where I come from or where I am going. You judge according to the flesh; I judge no one. Yet even if I do judge, my judgment is true, for it is not I alone who judge, but I and the Father who sent me. In your Law it is written that the testimony of two people is true. I am the one who bears witness about myself, and the Father who sent me bears witness about me." They said to him therefore, "Where is your Father?" Jesus answered, "You know neither me nor my Father. If you knew me, you would know my Father also." These words he spoke in the treasury, as he taught in the temple; but no one arrested him, because his hour had not yet come. (John 8:12-20)

Some accounts of the Feast of Booths tell us that four large menorahs were erected in the temple courtyard to light the area at night. The wicks, it was said, were made from worn-out linen garments worn by the priests. The light symbolized the pillar of light that led the Israelites through the wilderness (Exodus 13:21). After the return from exile, the Jews added the ceremony of the water and the menorahs to complement the temporary booths. Except for the booths, the two ceremonies were not commanded by God but likely became a custom for the celebration. John doesn't mention the menorahs, nor does any other gospel writer. If those lights were there in the temple at the time of Jesus, his words would have been an impressive and provocative proclamation.

Even without the light from the huge menorahs, his words were provocative: "I am the light of the world." To the Pharisees, Jesus was arrogant, blasphemous, and perhaps demented. C. S. Lewis said that you either have to believe Jesus or conclude that he was crazy. Throughout John's record of Jesus in the temple during the festival, we read that Jesus made one dramatic and provocative assertion after another. He claimed he had come from above—from God. He defended that assertion and said that the words he spoke came from God and had God's authority. He claimed to be the water that would create rivers of living water in those who believed him. Now he said, "I am the light of the world."

No wonder the Pharisees held so much animosity—no, hate—for Jesus. He was destroying their concept of God. He was demolishing the very foundations of what they believed to be true. This man who performed miracles and who spoke with such authority was claiming the authority of God. He bypassed their approval, their thinking, and their familiar practices. They had difficulty opposing him because he performed miracles of healing. Even some of those miracles that relieved suffering and disabilities were done on the Sabbath. That defied the Sabbath regulations, and yet Jesus defended what he had done.

They challenged Jesus by quoting a simple principle of law: "You are bearing witness about yourself." One must have corroborating testimony from someone or something else that validates or substantiates the assertion. Courts cannot convict on the assertion or accusation of one person.

Jesus defended himself with two arguments. The first was that these Pharisees were using human standards to judge him. Jesus claimed that his testimony was valid because he was not bound by human standards. He was above them. That's bold in any legal mind, but Jesus reminded them that he had claimed to come from above from God himself, who is above all human thinking and laws. He made the same claim now. God can do whatever he wills. The additional argument was that Jesus indeed is one who testifies for himself, that his other witness is his heavenly Father who sent him.

They want to know just who this second witness—the Father—is. Jesus' answer does not help them understand. They claimed to serve the Lord God of Israel. They celebrated this festival along with all the others. They read the Scriptures and followed all its regulations as precisely as possible. They could boast as the Pharisee in the parable did: "I thank [God] that I am not like other men. . . . I fast twice a week; I give tithes of all that I get" (Luke 18:11-12). Jesus boldly asserted, "You know neither me nor my Father." The God they served and worshiped with all their efforts was an illusion. They used the words of Scripture that were used for this and many other festivals. How often had they heard the words, "Our God is in the heavens; he does all that he pleases" (Psalm 115:3); "His steadfast love endures forever" (Psalm 118:1)? But they failed to grasp what these words meant as Jesus stood before them.

Here was Jesus in the temple courts openly proclaiming the love of God. Jesus was God's love in action. He was the one and only Son the Father chose to send to earth to die to take away the sins of the world and to rise again from the dead to gain victory over death. Jesus was about six months from the cross and empty tomb. The Jewish leaders wanted so badly to seize him and kill him, but his hour had not yet come. He would return and then fulfill what he had shared with his disciples.

PRAYER: Lord Jesus, you have shed your light in my heart. I have the light of life. I see that you are the one sent from above to rescue me from my sin and give me the assurance of eternal life with you. I trust your great love for me and all sinners. When so many around me think that your claims are preposterous and could not be true, let your light shine in my heart so I cling to your promises. Give me the courage and strength to share that light with those who still sit in darkness. Amen.

40

Who Are You?

[Jesus] said to them again, "I am going away, and you will seek me, and you will die in your sin. Where I am going, you cannot come." So the Jews said, "Will he kill himself, since he says, 'Where I am going, you cannot come'?" He said to them, "You are from below; I am from above. You are of this world; I am not of this world. I told you that you would die in your sins, for unless you believe that I am he you will die in your sins." So they said to him, "Who are you?" Jesus said to them, "Just what I have been telling you from the beginning. I have much to say about you and much to judge, but he who sent me is true, and I declare to the world what I have heard from him." They did not understand that he had been speaking to them about the Father. So Jesus said to them, "When you have lifted up the Son of Man, then you will know that I am he, and that I do nothing on my own authority, but speak just as the Father taught me. And he who sent me is with me. He has not left me alone, for I always do the things that are pleasing to him." As he was saying these things, many believed in him. (John 8:21-30)

Once more! How many times does Jesus have to say it? This time he repeats what he said during the festival: "I am going away." The first time he said this, the Jews thought Jesus meant he was going to travel to the Greeks and carry out his mission among them (John 7:35-36). It was a logical guess. If he went away to Greece, they could not follow. This time they speculated about another possibility. "Will he kill himself?" Once more they were unable to conceive anything beyond their knowledge and experience.

Jesus tells them why they were unable to understand: "You are from below; I am from above." His knowledge was not limited to the worlds of Galilee and Judea but stretched beyond to the glorious throne of God and eternity. Jesus set aside the glory of that throne above and entered the world below as a baby in Bethlehem. Then he grew up like all other humans to walk and talk in the world of those below.

John and the others—the Twelve and the others who believed in Jesus—did not fully grasp all the implications of what Jesus said. He would repeat the concept for them again in the upper room just before his passion. But after the crucifixion and resurrection, John would write at the beginning of his gospel, "In the beginning was the Word, and the Word was with God, and the Word was God. He was in the beginning with God. The Word became flesh and dwelt among us" (John 1:1-2,14). Jesus was from above. His message came from above. The mission the Father sent him to complete had its origin above.

But the critics of Jesus could think only of what made sense in this world. So their explanation was a trip to Greece or suicide. They could not imagine another explanation for his comment, "Where I am going, you cannot come." They would not accept what Jesus had been telling them during the festival. His message was a message of life and victory from above. He again said, "He who sent me is true, and I declare to the world what I have heard from him." His message was for the people of this world, but it was from the world beyond what they could see, taste, feel, or imagine. It was a message of the glory and majesty of heaven for all who believe.

Sadly, it is the same today. Those who do not believe cannot make sense of the message of Jesus. People today want scientific proof for the truth of the Scriptures. The miracles? Since there is no proof, they conclude that the miracles were invented by the followers of Jesus. Heaven? No one can prove it with the measurement tools of this world. What about the existence of God? He doesn't fit into a world that can think only of proving things by the standards, measurements, and tools of this world. So many people are confined to the here and now. They have no time for the otherworldly message of Jesus. It is impractical, unnecessary, and improbable.

"Who are you?" the critics of Jesus asked and still ask. What Jesus told them did not fit into their thinking because they were bound by the limitations of human experience and knowledge. They thought:

You look just like us; you talk just like us. Who are you that you can say these things about eternal life, forgiveness, and heaven?

Jesus understood their difficulty and explained his mission, hoping they might someday understand. "When you have lifted up the Son of Man, then you will know that I am he, and that I do nothing on my own authority, but speak just as the Father taught me." Many of these people would witness his crucifixion and resurrection. Then the light would begin to dawn on what Jesus had told them. After that, the disciples would go back to Jerusalem for another festival—Pentecost—and encourage the people to "repent and be baptized . . . in the name of Jesus Christ for the forgiveness of [their] sins" (Acts 2:38). The cross is the only thing that can break through the limitations of human thinking.

Even among these harsh and hard critics, many already believed. Is it any wonder that Jesus repeated his message once more? He was seeking the lost even in Jerusalem. It was a lesson for the disciples: Sow the seed of the Word. That's what Jesus told them to do, what he was teaching them here in Jerusalem, and what they would do after his resurrection. It's what we still do. Sow the Word and trust the Holy Spirit to change hearts.

PRAYER: Lord Jesus, I see so many around me who do not take time to listen to your truth. They have more important things to do and avoid the gospel outreach of my congregation, my own witness, and the witness of Scripture. Encourage all Christians to continue to share your truth in a world that doesn't care. Although some reject it, nevertheless, send your Spirit through their witness so that some will believe and be saved. Amen.

41

Believe His Word

Jesus said to the Jews who had believed him, "If you abide in my word, you are truly my disciples, and you will know the truth, and the truth will set you free." They answered him, "We are offspring of Abraham and have never been enslaved to anyone. How is it that you say, 'You will become free'?" Jesus answered them, "Truly, truly, I say to you, everyone who practices sin is a slave to sin. The slave does not remain in the house forever; the son remains forever. So if the Son sets you free, you will be free indeed. I know that you are offspring of Abraham; yet you seek to kill me because my word finds no place in you. I speak of what I have seen with my Father, and you do what you have heard from your father." They answered him, "Abraham is our father." Jesus said to them, "If you were Abraham's children, you would be doing the works Abraham did, but now you seek to kill me, a man who has told you the truth that I heard from God. This is not what Abraham did. You are doing the works your father did." They said to him, "We were not born of sexual immorality. We have one Father—even God." Jesus said to them, "If God were your Father, you would love me, for I came from God and I am here. I came not of my own accord, but he sent me. Why do you not understand what I say? It is because you cannot bear to hear my word. You are of your father the devil, and your will is to do your father's desires. He was a murderer from the beginning, and does not stand in the truth, because there is no truth in him. When he lies, he speaks out of his own character, for he is a liar and the father of lies. But because I tell the truth, you do not believe me. Which one of you convicts me of sin? If I tell the truth, why do you not believe me? Whoever is of God hears the words of God. The reason why you do not hear them is that you are not of God." (John 8:31-47)

Those who came to the festival looked for Jesus, but they did not speak about him publicly because they were afraid of their leaders. The leaders threatened that whoever spoke favorably of Jesus might be expelled from their synagogues. The people could not have missed the tension between their leaders and Jesus. The Pharisees especially attacked his ideas while everyone else listened. Jesus accused the Pharisees of trying to kill him. Then the leaders sent the temple officers to arrest Jesus. When Jesus made a provocative comment, they tried to seize him. In John chapters 7 and 8, the desire to seize Jesus is stated three times. It was a hostile environment for Jesus. Yet some believed him despite the threats and opposition.

Jesus encouraged the listeners, "If you abide in my word, you are truly my disciples." Holding to his teaching was the one standard for discipleship. "My word," he said, not the opinion of the Pharisees or the chief priests. Jesus had demonstrated that the Pharisees' opinions were only human opinions that obstructed the truth he was proclaiming. Discipleship was certainly not following blindly along with the ideas of the accepted crowd. It was holding on to the teachings of Jesus despite the opposition of other thoughts and ideas.

For us too, discipleship means trusting Jesus' words rather than the opinions of others. What Jesus has been saying here to his critics and to the believers is that his words are truth because they come from God above, from his Father and ours. Other ideas come from human intelligence and imagination. Some of them are brilliant and compelling, but they are not words that flow from God and his only begotten Son. Jesus tells all his disciples to recognize the difference and hold to his Word.

The Pharisees and other opponents of Jesus heard him speak. The disciples Jesus had gathered in the temple held to what Jesus said. In our age, one tactic of those who reject Jesus is to cast doubt on what Jesus said. They argue that these words were recorded long ago and may not be accurate. Some reject all of the Scriptures, and in scholarly books, conferences, and press releases they do what the Pharisees did in Jerusalem. They find it hard to swallow his words. Jesus identified the reason people would not accept his words: "My word finds no place in [them]." Their minds are closed to the idea that the words of Jesus are true. They view the record of Scripture as only human recollections written years later.

But the words of Jesus are true. The record we have comes from the time immediately after Jesus ascended. Those who wrote were "eyewitnesses," as Peter said (2 Peter 1:16). Luke wrote his gospel after "having followed all things closely for some time past" (Luke 1:3). In many ways we are these disciples in the temple. We may be confronted with arguments and opposition different from those they were confronted with, but the world still has no room for God's Word. Each age will face its own opposition to Jesus, but disciples of every age and era know that discipleship is holding on to the teaching of Jesus and abandoning the ideas of others.

The reason is simple. He came here from God and "has told [us] the truth that [he] heard from God." The words of Jesus are not the words or concepts of just another philosopher or thinker. Disciples know the difference, and "whoever is of God hears the words of God." There's another reason. When we know the words of Jesus and hold to them, we are set free. We are released from the slavery of following every new and innovative idea only to realize that it only makes room for the next new and innovative idea. It's a never-ending cycle of human thinking. However, the words of Jesus endure and have endured through the ages.

PRAYER: Lord Jesus, not only am I constantly confronted by those who oppose you and your words, but because I am still a sinful creature, I also find a weakness within my own heart that questions and doubts your Word. Keep me from whatever draws me away from your Word and enslaves me. Strengthen me as your disciple to hold to your teachings and to read and meditate on those words that grant me freedom from sin and death. Amen.

42

I Am

The Jews answered [Jesus,] "Are we not right in saying that you are a Samaritan and have a demon?" Jesus answered, "I do not have a demon, but I honor my Father, and you dishonor me. Yet I do not seek my own glory; there is One who seeks it, and he is the judge. Truly, truly, I say to you, if anyone keeps my word, he will never see death." The Jews said to him, "Now we know that you have a demon! Abraham died, as did the prophets, yet you say, 'If anyone keeps my word, he will never taste death.' Are you greater than our father Abraham, who died? And the prophets died! Who do you make yourself out to be?" Jesus answered, "If I glorify myself, my glory is nothing. It is my Father who glorifies me, of whom you say, 'He is our God.' But you have not known him. I know him. If I were to say that I do not know him, I would be a liar like you, but I do know him and I keep his word. Your father Abraham rejoiced that he would see my day. He saw it and was glad." So the Jews said to him, "You are not yet fifty years old, and have you seen Abraham?" Jesus said to them, "Truly, truly, I say to you, before Abraham was, I am." So they picked up stones to throw at him, but Jesus hid himself and went out of the temple. (John 8:48-59)

What did the disciples of Jesus learn during this extended dialogue with the Jews? Jesus was at the festival as the obedient Son of his heavenly Father. He was perfectly obedient for all who were imperfect—every sinner. But he was also at the festival to engage the Jews and assert his origin and, therefore, the truth of his words. He had come from above to proclaim the truth he had heard from God (John 8:40). What did the disciples learn as they listened and watched?

The disciples already knew that Jesus was, as Peter confessed, "the Christ, the Son of the living God" (Matthew 16:16). That lesson was confirmed here by the bold assertions of Jesus. They learned what they had sensed earlier from the encounters with the Pharisees over the past years. Serious opposition to Jesus was alive and well in Jerusalem. The hatred and hard opposition of the Jews filled the air with crackling electricity. The give-and-take was ongoing and relentless. The lesson was clear: Jesus would not only be rejected; he already was rejected by the Jewish leaders.

But there was a positive lesson too. The disciples watched and learned from Jesus' demeanor as he responded to bitter opposition. He did not show anger and call down fire and brimstone on his enemies. He was patient but firm and frank and outspoken. Peter clearly expressed the lesson he learned from Jesus: "Always being prepared to make a defense to anyone who asks you for a reason for the hope that is in you; yet do it with gentleness and respect, having a good conscience, so that, when you are slandered, those who revile your good behavior in Christ may be put to shame" (1 Peter 3:15-16). Jesus was teaching his disciples and preparing them for the days ahead when he would not be visibly present. Then they would have to be the sowers of the gospel in a world that opposed him, his message, and them.

As the disciples listened, they would have also learned that Jesus spoke to four distinct audiences. The first was the most obvious. He spoke to his enemies with candor and firmness. They were like the seed that fell on the hard ground that the birds came and quickly ate. They plotted to kill him. At the same time, Jesus continued to speak the truth to them and included some harsh warnings. He exposed their plot to kill him, called them children of their father, the devil, and warned them that they would die in their sins if they did not repent.

The second audience included those convinced by his words. They believed in him, and he encouraged them to hold on to his teaching and be his disciples even in the face of opposition. The third audience included those who were on the fence and needed more time and encouragement to believe in him. They may have left the festival still not committed to Jesus, but they would return to other festivals, perhaps Pentecost, and learn of the importance of the Savior's crucifixion and resurrection. Then they would believe—three thousand in one day. Jerusalem would eventually be the site of a large collection of believers. Perhaps some in the second and third groups would be like the seed that fell among the thorns or on the rocky soil, but other seed would fall on good ground and eventually sprout and bear the fruits of faith.

The fourth audience was the disciples who came with Jesus to the festival. They were committed to him even though they were still unclear about his mission. Jesus confirmed their devotion. They may have been puzzled when Jesus said he would suffer, be rejected by the elders and teachers, and be killed. But, except for one, they were hard-core believers. Like many others, they would not understand everything until Jesus rose from the dead. Then the Holy Spirit would help them put all the pieces together and give them the courage to "speak the word of God with boldness" (Acts 4:31).

Near the end of the dialogue, Jesus proclaimed, "Truly, truly, I say to you, if anyone keeps my word, he will never see death." Those who opposed Jesus thought that claim was outrageous and ridiculous. Everyone knew that Abraham and the prophets all had died. So they responded sarcastically, "You are not yet fifty years old, and have you seen Abraham?"

In the response of Jesus, all four audiences heard one of the clearest declarations of his identity: "Before Abraham was, I am." His opponents quickly understood that Jesus was saying he was God—the God who appeared to Moses and said, "I AM WHO I AM. . . . Say this to the people of Israel: 'I AM has sent me to you'" (Exodus 3:14). They had stones in hand and were ready to kill Jesus, but he slipped away from the temple grounds. To the others, this response confirmed and clarified what he had been saying from the first.

PRAYER: Lord, you have sent me to sow the seed of your gospel in my world and among those who do not know you. Give me courage to speak. Grant me clarity when I struggle to speak the truth. Fill me with love for those who need to hear your gospel. Grant me boldness to speak, but keep me gentle and kind with firmness in the hope of your great promises. Amen.

43

I Believe

As [Jesus] passed by, he saw a man blind from birth. And his disciples asked him, "Rabbi, who sinned, this man or his parents, that he was born blind?" Jesus answered, "It was not that this man sinned, or his parents, but that the works of God might be displayed in him. We must work the works of him who sent me while it is day; night is coming, when no one can work. As long as I am in the world, I am the light of the world." Having said these things, he spit on the ground and made mud with the saliva. Then he anointed the man's eyes with the mud and said to him, "Go, wash in the pool of Siloam" (which means Sent). So he went and washed and came back seeing. They brought to the Pharisees the man who had formerly been blind. Now it was a Sabbath day when Jesus made the mud and opened his eyes. Some of the Pharisees said, "This man is not from God, for he does not keep the Sabbath." But others said, "How can a man who is a sinner do such signs?" And there was a division among them. He answered, "Whether he is a sinner I do not know. One thing I do know, that though I was blind, now I see." They said to him, "What did he do to you? How did he open your eyes?" He answered them, "I have told you already, and you would not listen. Why do you want to hear it again? Do you also want to become his disciples?" And they reviled him, saying, "You are his disciple, but we are disciples of Moses. We know that God has spoken to Moses, but as for this man, we do not know where he comes from." The man answered, "Why, this is an amazing thing! You do not know where he comes from, and yet he opened my eyes. We know that God does not listen to sinners, but if anyone is a worshiper of God and does his will, God listens to him. Never since the world began has it been heard that anyone opened the eyes of a man born blind. If this man were not from God, he could do nothing." They answered him, "You were born in utter sin, and would you teach us?" And they cast him out. Jesus heard that they had cast him out, and having found him he said, "Do you believe in the Son of Man?" He answered, "And who is he, sir, that I may believe in him?" Jesus said to him, "You have seen him, and it is he who is speaking to you." He said, "Lord, I believe," and he worshiped him. (John 9:1-7,13-14,16,25-38)

Sometimes deeds are better than words. Or at least sometimes deeds prove words are true and reliable. Jesus left the temple grounds and saw a man who had been blind from birth—a reality that had no remedy in the ancient world. What follows in this chapter proved that Jesus was from above. He did what no one else could do.

Some in our world today dismiss this miracle as a later embellishment that makes Jesus look good. Those who reject the Jesus we find in the Scriptures think this story, among so many that point to Jesus as true God, was added much later. Some suggest it was added perhaps near A.D. 300 near the time of the Council of Nicaea, which asserted that Jesus is "God from God, Light from Light, true God from true God." Still others simply dismiss it because it is a miracle, and miracles didn't happen because they cannot be proven to have taken place.

Jesus paused with his disciples when they saw this man. The disciples had a question and were looking for a simple way to process the tragedy. There must be some reason for his blindness, and they concluded that the reason must be either that he did some grievous sin or his parents had done something to deserve it. Jesus corrected them. A specific sin by this man or his parents was not responsible. Instead, it was an opportunity to display the gracious and loving work of God. Then Jesus made a paste with the ground and his spit, applied it to the man's eyes, and told him, "Go, wash in the pool of Siloam."

Jesus and his disciples went on their way, but the miracle blazed a path through this man's neighbors and those who had seen him begging. They could not believe what had happened. The man said that Jesus had healed him, but no one knew where Jesus was. That was a problem. The path that the miracle blazed led to the Pharisees because Jesus healed the man on the Sabbath.

The Pharisees didn't believe it was possible for a man born blind to see. It must have been a fraud. Was he really blind from birth? They explored that question with the man's parents. But their opposition to Jesus blinded them to the possibility that Jesus could heal the man. Earlier they were blind to the truth of Jesus' comments about doing good on the Sabbath. They concluded that Jesus was not from God but was a sinner. When the man who had been healed objected, the Pharisees "reviled" him and asserted their superiority: "You were born in utter sin, and would you teach us?"

The Pharisees hadn't changed. The miracle demonstrated the truth of Jesus' claim. Even after investigating it, they were the blind ones. They threw the man out. But Jesus did not forget him. He sought him out in order to draw him closer to the truth. The unnamed blind man believed and worshiped Jesus. Jesus' miracle confirmed the truth, and the man believed—"Lord, I believe"—no longer blind physically or spiritually.

PRAYER: Jesus, you are Lord and can do all things. Those who were eyewitnesses to your presence here on earth tell us that you used your power to help and heal others. Like the Pharisees long ago, many still find reasons to dismiss your miracles and to remain blind—a blindness that cannot see you as Lord of all and Savior from sin, death, and hell. Keep me faithful to your Word. Draw me closer to you when I am confused by the world around me. I believe, Lord. Keep my faith in you strong. Amen.

44

The Gatekeeper and the Shepherd

"Truly, truly, I say to you, he who does not enter the sheepfold by the door but climbs in by another way, that man is a thief and a robber. But he who enters by the door is the shepherd of the sheep. To him the gatekeeper opens. The sheep hear his voice, and he calls his own sheep by name and leads them out. When he has brought out all his own, he goes before them, and the sheep follow him, for they know his voice. A stranger they will not follow, but they will flee from him, for they do not know the voice of strangers." This figure of speech Jesus used with them, but they did not understand what he was saying to them. So Jesus again said to them, "Truly, truly, I say to you, I am the door of the sheep. All who came before me are thieves and robbers, but the sheep did not listen to them. I am the door. If anyone enters by me, he will be saved and will go in and out and find pasture. The thief comes only to steal and kill and destroy. I came that they may have life and have it abundantly." (John 10:1-10)

Jesus had repeated again and again that he was sent from God. On the last day of the festival, he proclaimed, "I am the light of the world" (John 8:12). After that, the discussion continued, perhaps on the temple steps. The Pharisees were not satisfied with the answers Jesus gave. Repeatedly, they had sought to seize Jesus, but they could not. When Jesus claimed, "Before Abraham was, I am" (John 8:58), they picked up stones to kill him, but Jesus slipped away from the temple grounds without one stone being launched in his direction. The long, sharp exchanges during the Feast of Booths had come to an end.

Then the miracle of the man born blind frustrated the Pharisees. Jesus demonstrated in a dramatic way that he had the power and authority to be and do what he said—to give sight to the blind. But he also gave the man he healed a second kind of sight: The man saw Jesus as the one sent by God. His spiritual eyes were opened, and he believed. Sadly, the miracle did not open the eyes of the Pharisees. Even though they could see, they remained blind. They refused to see Jesus as the one sent by God, and Jesus reminded them of that.

After the miracle, these last words of Jesus in Jerusalem were remarkable. We still treasure these words and find great strength and comfort in them. In a beautiful figure of speech, an allegory of sorts, Jesus told the Pharisees once again who he was and why he came. We note two parts to his comments. One part speaks of the relationship between the gatekeeper and the shepherd. Jesus clearly identified the mission he had spoken of in Nazareth when he read from Isaiah, "The Spirit of the Lord God is upon me, because the LORD has anointed me to bring good news to the poor" (Isaiah 61:1). Since that time, Jesus had proclaimed the truth in Galilee, Tyre and Sidon, Decapolis, and most recently in Jerusalem at the Feast of Booths.

At the festival in Jerusalem, he clearly and often said that he had come from God with God's message. He said, "I came not of my own accord, but he sent me" (John 8:42) and "I declare to the world what I have heard from him" (John 8:26). Through that long dialogue with the Pharisees, Jesus identified himself as "a man who has told you the truth that I heard from God" (John 8:40).

The second part of the Savior's comment tells the Pharisees and us what the true Shepherd does. His task is to call his sheep to himself. The sheep know the voice and message of the Shepherd and follow him. They run from strangers because they do not recognize the voices of strangers. Throughout the years of his ministry, Jesus has been speaking to his sheep and caring for them. He knows them by name and is tenderly concerned about them, and they follow him. Some followed him to Jerusalem. Even in Jerusalem, many found in his voice the gentle voice of a caring Shepherd and believed. He led them too. We too have heard his voice and follow him.

This Shepherd is the one with the truth. He is the gate—the entrance to the truth. "If anyone enters by me, he will be saved." There is no other way—no other source of truth. Others are imposters who come to steal, kill, and destroy. He is the one, the only one, who can promise, "I came that they may have life and have it abundantly." All because he has come from God with God's own message to proclaim.

As tender and important as these words are for his sheep, Jesus warns the Pharisees. They have rejected the one true Shepherd whom God sent. Perhaps the reference to the shepherd brought to the minds of these biblical scholars in Jerusalem the prophet Ezekiel, who wrote, "Ah, shepherds of Israel who have been feeding yourselves! I will require my sheep at their hand and put a stop to their feeding the sheep. No longer shall the shepherds feed themselves. I will rescue my sheep from their mouths, that they may not be food for them. . . . I myself will search for my sheep and will seek them out. I myself will be the shepherd of my sheep, and I myself will make them lie down, declares the Lord GOD" (Ezekiel 34:2,10-11,15). So Jesus appeared to proclaim good news and tend the flock as the Good Shepherd—a fulfillment of God's promise. But the Pharisees did not understand this any more than they understood anything Jesus had said before.

PRAYER: Dear Shepherd, your voice has called me to follow you. Your voice gives me strength and hope when I am weak and lost. It gives me comfort when I have none and joy when I am filled with pain. I hear your voice promise eternal life and peace. I feel your hand gently lift me when I stumble. In my anguish you point my eyes forward to see your gracious promises of glory. Continue, dear Shepherd, to speak words of love to me and strengthen me to follow when I am weary. For your glory's sake. Amen.

45

Good Shepherd

"I am the good shepherd. The good shepherd lays down his life for the sheep. He who is a hired hand and not a shepherd, who does not own the sheep, sees the wolf coming and leaves the sheep and flees, and the wolf snatches them and scatters them. He flees because he is a hired hand and cares nothing for the sheep. I am the good shepherd. I know my own and my own know me, just as the Father knows me and I know the Father; and I lay down my life for the sheep. And I have other sheep that are not of this fold. I must bring them also, and they will listen to my voice. So there will be one flock, one shepherd. For this reason the Father loves me, because I lay down my life that I may take it up again. No one takes it from me, but I lay it down of my own accord. I have authority to lay it down, and I have authority to take it up again. This charge I have received from my Father." There was again a division among the Jews because of these words. Many of them said, "He has a demon, and is insane; why listen to him?" Others said, "These are not the words of one who is oppressed by a demon. Can a demon open the eyes of the blind?" (John 10:11-21)

During the three years of his ministry, Jesus traveled and taught. He performed miracles—some of them in relative privacy but some of them in large crowds like the feeding of the five thousand. The crowds had gathered to hear his message. He was like the shepherd who gathered his sheep as Jesus had just explained to the Pharisees. In this last year, the year of opposition, Jesus focused on teaching his disciples. That included more than just the Twelve. He avoided Judea until the end of September for the Feast of Booths. Then in Jerusalem at the festival he continued to teach and gather his sheep in the face of stiff opposition from the Pharisees.

Jesus' words about the gatekeeper and the shepherd appear to be the last words he spoke while in Jerusalem at this time. Some in the crowd were still buzzing with the miracle of the blind man. Jesus was about to leave Jerusalem and continue his ministry of proclaiming the good news in Perea, across the Jordan River. Mark tells us, "Crowds gathered to him again. And again, as was his custom, he taught them" (Mark 10:1).

But before he left Jerusalem, he had one more important and critical point to make. "I am the good shepherd. The good shepherd lays down his life for the sheep." This declaration was in keeping with what Jesus had told his disciples about his suffering, death, and resurrection. On one level, it was easy to understand that Jesus the Good Shepherd would lay down his life for the sheep. In Jerusalem the angry crowd sought to seize him more than once. They had picked up stones to kill him.

The sacrifice of the Good Shepherd was yet to come. He would lay down his life for the sheep at the time appointed. His sacrifice would flow from his love for the sheep. He knows his sheep, loves them dearly, and says he willingly lays down his life for the sheep. The disciples had heard this theme before but did not understand.

Now Jesus announced his sacrifice in the face of opposition by the Pharisees and chief priests. But his sacrifice was not an inevitable event over which he had no control. It was a loving sacrifice. He had the authority to lay down his life. It was for that very reason that he had come to earth. Yes, he came to proclaim the good news. But there was more to his mission. He came to die and complete the plan he had been given by his heavenly Father.

Jesus was not surprised by the opposition or the prospect of his own death. He knew from the beginning what would happen. Isaiah foretold it all long ago: "All we like sheep have gone astray; we have turned—every one—to his own way; and the LORD has laid on him the iniquity of us all. By oppression and judgment he was taken away; and as for his generation, who considered that he was cut off out of the land of the living, stricken for the transgression of my people?" (Isaiah 53:6,8).

The Pharisees sought the death of Jesus because they thought it would end his influence. Then his disciples could be rounded up and eliminated. After all, they were only uneducated Galileans. The ministry of Jesus would simply be a short sentence in their history. But Jesus would not die because the Pharisees plotted his death. Jesus said instead, "I lay [my life] down of my own accord." His death would not silence him. His death would bring many others—his other sheep—to the truth he proclaimed. They would also hear his voice and become his followers. The ministry of Jesus, including the death of Jesus, was for all and created one flock under one Shepherd. Here Jesus predicts the growth of his church, extending it to all nations and peoples.

"I lay down my life that I may take it up again." As the great I AM he could say that. He carried out the plan given to him by his Father: teaching, dying, and rising again. At this point, perhaps no one understood what the resurrection was. The disciples didn't grasp it fully even when it happened. Jesus had to expand the lesson as he did with the two men on the road to Emmaus. His death and resurrection form the foundation of our faith. We know now what Jesus meant and we rejoice: Jesus laid down his life and took it up again. He died for us all and rose again for our justification.

PRAYER: Lord Jesus, you willingly laid down your life for me and all humanity so that our sins might be punished in your suffering and death. You proclaimed from the cross, "It is finished" (John 19:30). Then you rose again to assure us all that we will live as you promised. Praise, honor, thanks, and glory be to you. Keep us always as precious sheep in your pasture that you purchased with your blood. Amen.

46

Male and Female

[Jesus] left there and went to the region of Judea and beyond the Jordan, and crowds gathered to him again. And again, as was his custom, he taught them. And Pharisees came up and in order to test him asked, "Is it lawful for a man to divorce his wife?" He answered them, "What did Moses command you?" They said, "Moses allowed a man to write a certificate of divorce and to send her away." And Jesus said to them, "Because of your hardness of heart he wrote you this commandment. But from the beginning of creation, 'God made them male and female.' 'Therefore a man shall leave his father and mother and hold fast to his wife, and the two shall become one flesh.' So they are no longer two but one flesh. What therefore God has joined together, let not man separate." And in the house the disciples asked him again about this matter. And he said to them, "Whoever divorces his wife and marries another commits adultery against her, and if she divorces her husband and marries another, she commits adultery." (Mark 10:1-12)

Heading away from Jerusalem didn't mean that Jesus was walking away humiliated with his head bowed and without followers. Among the crowds he attracted were those who were ready to follow him wherever he went, as one confessed. Jesus did not abandon his mission to "proclaim good news" (Luke 4:18). Instead of being shamed into silence by the vehement opposition of the Pharisees, "as was his custom . . . he taught" the crowds. He was no longer in Galilee or Jerusalem but in the area where John the Baptist had announced the coming of the Messiah. John had pointed to Jesus and proclaimed, "Behold, the Lamb of God!" (John 1:36). Now Jesus turned his attention to this part of Judea to carry out the remaining months of his ministry.

Jesus refused to stop teaching, and the Pharisees did not stop opposing him. Again, some came and tested him. The question is provocative: "Is it lawful for a man to divorce his wife?" Divorce is a troubling failure of one man and one woman to continue the relationship they promised when they took the vows of marriage. The trouble is not unique to our age even though we see multiple divorces and remarriages. The question asked so long ago has changed only a little. Now, identifying whether a husband can divorce his wife, we ask if a woman can divorce her husband. The question for us today is "Is it lawful to get a divorce?"

The answer to the question today—and no doubt at the time of Jesus—is keenly awaited. Men and women are not perfect. Both bring faults and weaknesses to their relationship in marriage. Who would Jesus say was right to divorce and who was wrong? The blame game is not a modern invention of interpersonal relationships. What makes this question even more important is that the Pharisees were asking Jesus, who was widely respected for his teaching. He claimed to be the one sent from heaven and claimed to be God, the "I AM" of Exodus (John 8:58).

The Pharisees asked Jesus in front of a crowd that, no doubt, included more than a few who were divorced or knew people who were divorced. It was a difficult question that even the Jewish rabbis had trouble answering, with some on one side and others on the other side. Jesus' answer had the potential to undermine his message and make enemies of one side or the other. Some in the crowd would turn away if he condemned divorce. Others would turn away if he condoned divorce. The question today has the same potential.

Jesus directed the Pharisees to Moses (Deuteronomy 24:1-4) and asked what God commanded about divorce. "Moses allowed a man to write a certificate of divorce," they responded. Why did God's law allow divorce? Jesus left no doubt: "Because of your hardness of heart he wrote you this commandment." Jesus said what is common sense but avoided by many who confront the deterioration of their marriage. Repairing the marriage relationship must often confront the harsh reality of entrenched feelings and ideas that become immovable objects—the hearts, sometimes of both husband and wife, become hard.

Jesus took one more step in his answer. He went to the beginning of creation. God did not intend heartache, deception, bitterness, or anger for his creatures. The man and woman, Adam and Eve, were created perfect for each other, and God intended that every marriage would be patterned on the same mutual respect, love, and concern (Genesis 2:18-25). The two were to join together and be one flesh, establishing a new relationship different from the relationship to parents. It was to be a lifelong union, unbroken by unfaithfulness or other faults that would breed bitterness and lead to divorce. Adultery was one reason to dissolve the relationship of marriage. The apostle Paul offered another: desertion of the vow to love, honor, and cherish each other.

Jesus' answer to the question identifies the core problem in marriage—sin, or the hardness of the human heart. Adam and Eve brought it into the world with their disobedience. We see how it troubled the marriage relationship when God confronted them both. They hid for shame, blamed God, and pointed the finger of guilt at someone else. Troubled marriages often begin with flaws and build to something more sinister, including domestic violence.

The cure, even in this imperfect world with its sharply ragged edges, in marriage too is the Lamb of God. He came to assume the guilt for all sins and pay the penalty for all. His blood cleanses every sin, and his forgiveness changes hearts. A husband and wife—headed for divorce—can recognize the great forgiveness Jesus gives them both and can even then forgive each other for the angry words and thoughtless unfaithfulness. Unfortunately, sometimes that is not possible, especially with adultery. Then God allows the innocent partner to set aside the sins in his or her total forgiveness and build a new life—to turn the page and move on.

PRAYER: Lord, I know that sin lurks within my heart, waiting for an opportunity to spring to life and pollute and destroy all my relationships. Temptation becomes an ally of the sin inside. Remind me often of your forgiveness and love so that I may drown the sin within and oppose every temptation. Help me to lead a chaste and decent life in word and deed so that I do not spoil your loving gifts of spouse and children. In your name, Lord Jesus. Amen.

47

Little Children

They were bringing children to [Jesus] that he might touch them, and the disciples rebuked them. But when Jesus saw it, he was indignant and said to them, "Let the children come to me; do not hinder them, for to such belongs the kingdom of God. Truly, I say to you, whoever does not receive the kingdom of God like a child shall not enter it." And he took them in his arms and blessed them, laying his hands on them. (Mark 10:13-16)

Mark places this event in Perea, after the discussion about divorce and marriage. Matthew does the same. The crowds were still drawn to Jesus. Apparently, the question about divorce did not have the effect the Pharisees had hoped for. Instead, a natural progression occurred from marriage to children. In the beginning when God created Adam and Eve, he said, "Be fruitful and multiply" (Genesis 1:22). As God intended, the intimate relationship of marriage resulted in children. In a perfect world, all relationships would be without argument and tension, and children would flourish in such loving relationships.

As Jesus had gone back to the beginning to sanctify marriage as part of God's plan, naturally those faithful to their spouses thought of the blessing God had given them—their children. They wanted the blessing of Jesus on their children. As both Matthew and Mark tell us, parents brought little children. Matthew mentions that they desired Jesus both to pray for these children and to bless them.

The interruption of these parents with their children was not a welcome one for the disciples. At times the disciples seem to have served as a kind of security force around Jesus, screening those who came close and preventing others from seeing him. Perhaps that was understandable since the Pharisees in Jerusalem sought to stone Jesus or seize him. Jesus, of course, was in control, but the disciples, understandably, were loyal and protective.

Yet their effort to screen Jesus from the children was a step too far. They rebuked the parents who brought their little ones to Jesus. To them, the questions from the crowd, including those of the Pharisees, were more important. They thought these children were interrupting the teaching ministry of Jesus. But Jesus was *indignant*, a nice-sounding word for "angry." Yes, Jesus was angry with his disciples. They were keeping children away from his loving touch and tender blessings.

Jesus firmly corrected them: "Let the children come to me; do not hinder them." The children were precious blessings God had given these parents. They wanted nothing but the best for their little ones, so they brought them to Jesus for his blessings and prayers. The word Jesus used here includes young children—little ones—those who could not walk yet but were carried by their mothers and who suckled at their mother's breasts.

Jesus had used a child to shame the disciples when they argued over who was the greatest. Placing the child before them, he said, "Truly, I say to you, unless you turn and become like children, you will never enter the kingdom of heaven" (Matthew 18:3). That lesson was difficult for the disciples to learn. Perhaps they had forgotten.

Jesus took the lesson here one step further: "For to such belongs the kingdom of God." Earlier, a child had been a lesson in humility, and now Jesus gave a pointed reminder that the kingdom of God is for children—little children. Simple, humble trust is the key to the kingdom. The disciples forgot, but a look at the children in their mothers' arms or standing and holding on to a father's garment carried an important lesson. Children in their mother's arms could look expectantly at her face, expecting love, attention, protection, and nourishment. Simple faith. Trust. Consider the children who held their father's garment. Those children felt secure, protected, and loved. The love of both mother and father had brought these little ones to Jesus.

The lesson ought not be lost on us. When we are so filled with our own importance, we should think of little children and the simple trust they have for everything they need at that moment. We are children of our heavenly Father. He gives us all we need. Most important, he gives us his undeserved love. Like an infant trusting the love of a parent, we trust the love of our heavenly Father. His love for us has brought him here as a little child in Joseph and Mary's care. He grew up to be the teacher of these children. He shared his love for them, picked them up in his arms, placed his hands on them, and blessed them.

"Do not hinder them." "Let the children come." Do not forget what was ahead for Jesus. Perhaps fewer than six months after this, he would be in Jerusalem, bloody and beaten. He had come to give his life for these little ones—and for all humanity—to cleanse them, their parents, and all of us. The kingdom of God belongs to these little ones as well as us adults. These little ones can trust their heavenly Father, and we need to remember to trust the same heavenly Father with the same kind of complete and simple trust. Don't hinder the children from coming to Jesus. Put away your pretensions, your worries, your doubts. Trust. It's what every child of God needs to do no matter the age.

PRAYER: I, a child, Lord Jesus, come to you asking you to help me trust you without doubt or question. At times I think the kingdom is nothing by comparison to the power and glory of this world. I sometimes even measure the success of your kingdom by what I do in the kingdom. Teach me the lesson I so often forget. Your kingdom is measured by all those—young and old—who simply and humbly trust in you. Keep me as such a child, for your name's sake. Amen.

48

Hard for the Rich

As [Jesus] was setting out on his journey, a man ran up and knelt before him and asked him, "Good Teacher, what must I do to inherit eternal life?" And Jesus said to him, "Why do you call me good? No one is good except God alone. You know the commandments: 'Do not murder, Do not commit adultery, Do not steal, Do not bear false witness, Do not defraud, Honor your father and mother.'" And he said to him, "Teacher, all these I have kept from my youth." And Jesus, looking at him, loved him, and said to him, "You lack one thing: go, sell all that you have and give to the poor, and you will have treasure in heaven; and come, follow me." Disheartened by the saying, he went away sorrowful, for he had great possessions. And Jesus looked around and said to his disciples, "How difficult it will be for those who have wealth to enter the kingdom of God!" And the disciples were amazed at his words. But Jesus said to them again, "Children, how difficult it is to enter the kingdom of God! It is easier for a camel to go through the eye of a needle than for a rich person to enter the kingdom of God." And they were exceedingly astonished, and said to him, "Then who can be saved?" Jesus looked at them and said, "With man it is impossible, but not with God. For all things are possible with God." (Mark 10:17-27)

Jesus put the last little child back into a mother's caring arms and began to walk on. As he walked away, a man ran after him with a question. "Good Teacher," he said, "what must I do to inherit eternal life?" He called Jesus "Good Teacher," so he must have watched and listened to Jesus before. He asked the question because he was confident that Jesus had the answer. His question was not meant to trap Jesus but came from a sincere heart addressed to someone he believed knew the answer.

Jesus reminded him of a fundamental truth: "No one is good except God alone." Was the man familiar with David, who was guilty of adultery and murder? Did he remember what David wrote? "Behold, I was brought forth in iniquity, and in sin did my mother conceive me. Behold, you delight in truth in the inward being" (Psalm 51:5-6). Perhaps he did not know what David had said. Had he also forgotten what the good God had said about sin? "Your iniquities have made a separation between you and your God" (Isaiah 59:2).

We recognize our iniquities by comparing them with the commandments of God. Jesus listed a few. Perhaps the man looked at Jesus quizzically. He didn't understand and said, "Teacher, all these I have kept from my youth." Although he was sincere, respectful, and concerned about the truth, he knew nothing of his unworthiness before God. Jesus could have reminded him what Isaiah confessed about all humans, "We have all become like one who is unclean, and all our righteous deeds are like a polluted garment" (Isaiah 64:6). Instead, Jesus looked at this young man with the eyes of love. Jesus longed for the man's repentance.

Jesus provided a way for the man to confront what he was not ready to yet. He said, "You lack one thing: go, sell all that you have and give to the poor, and you will have treasure in heaven; and come, follow me." Jesus perceived that this man's wealth was preventing him from seeing how far he was from the good God of heaven. His life was full of wealth; he had no room for anything else. As long as he felt that he had no sin and kept the commandments, he needed no Savior. What Jesus told him to do required more than he was willing to learn. His wealth left no room in his life for the answer to his question.

The inheritance of eternal life is a gracious gift of God to his children. It cannot be earned or bought. It is for all—rich and poor, young and old, men and women. Those who believe and trust Jesus just as little children trust their dear parents are children of God and heirs of eternal life. How hard it was for this man to have such trust. His priority was his great wealth, not Jesus, even though he came to seek the road to eternal life from Jesus. He walked away. His wealth was too great a barrier.

Jesus turned to his disciples and said, "How difficult it will be for those who have wealth to enter the kingdom of God!" That lesson amazed them. This man was different from the Pharisees and teachers of the law. He was sincere in his question. He wanted to inherit eternal life. Jesus had invited all to come to him. The crowds of people who came to him wanted rest for their souls. Why did this man walk away? Jesus had just taught them about little children and the kingdom of God. Those who trusted God were little children and inherited eternal life.

The disciples' amazement did not end. They realized what kept people from eternal life. It was a heart and life too full to make room for Jesus and his promise of eternal life. Such a heart felt no need for forgiveness or grace. This man felt he had kept all the commandments. Jesus tried to break into that heart, suggesting that the man's wealth left no room for God or eternal life. The man had made wealth more important, so he had no room for a humble childlike faith in Jesus. It's not just money that does it. Many fill their hearts with so much that there is no room for the faith needed to inherit eternal life. "Then who can be saved?"

Saving ourselves is impossible. Only God can give eternal life. No one will inherit eternal life on personal merits or because he or she is good enough. That's what Jesus wanted the rich man to understand. In addition, no human can even choose eternal life on his or her own. Only God can draw us to abandon whatever priorities fill our hearts and prevent us from trusting him. He draws us simply with his Word—law and gospel. The law shows us our sin and need for a Savior. The gospel extends God's promises and invites us to believe like little children. Jesus said so clearly, "God so loved the world, that he gave his only Son, that whoever believes in him should not perish but have eternal life" (John 3:16).

PRAYER: Lord, I too have come to you asking how to inherit eternal life. I have no list of deeds long enough or good enough to merit such an inheritance. I have failed to live a perfect life. Yet I raise my voice in praise and thanks that you have adopted me as your child by grace through your suffering, death, and resurrection. I am your child by grace and therefore inherit eternal life as you have promised. Help me treasure the wonder of your grace. Amen.

49

My Sheep

At that time the Feast of Dedication took place at Jerusalem. It was winter, and Jesus was walking in the temple, in the colonnade of Solomon. So the Jews gathered around him and said to him, "How long will you keep us in suspense? If you are the Christ, tell us plainly." Jesus answered them, "I told you, and you do not believe. The works that I do in my Father's name bear witness about me, but you do not believe because you are not among my sheep. My sheep hear my voice, and I know them, and they follow me. I give them eternal life, and they will never perish, and no one will snatch them out of my hand. My Father, who has given them to me, is greater than all, and no one is able to snatch them out of the Father's hand. I and the Father are one." The Jews picked up stones again to stone him. Jesus answered them, "I have shown you many good works from the Father; for which of them are you going to stone me?" The Jews answered him, "It is not for a good work that we are going to stone you but for blasphemy, because you, being a man, make yourself God." Jesus answered them, "Is it not written in your Law, 'I said, you are gods'? If he called them gods to whom the word of God came—and Scripture cannot be broken—do you say of him whom the Father consecrated and sent into the world, 'You are blaspheming,' because I said, 'I am the Son of God'? If I am not doing the works of my Father, then do not believe me; but if I do them, even though you do not believe me, believe the works, that you may know and understand that the Father is in me and I am in the Father." Again they sought to arrest him, but he escaped from their hands. (John 10:22-39)

John wrote that it was the Feast of Dedication (Hanukkah, or the Festival of Lights) and it was winter. The festival celebrated the rededication of the temple at the time of the Maccabean Revolt in the second century B.C. Jesus returned to Jerusalem for the festival in late December.

John's comments about the Feast of Booths (John 7) and the Feast of Dedication here give us a timetable for the last months of Jesus' ministry. The Feast of Booths occurred in mid-October and the Feast of Dedication in late December. Between those festivals Jesus concentrated his ministry in Perea. After Hanukkah, John wrote that Jesus "went away again across the Jordan" (John 10:40) and resumed his work in Perea. That places this incident about three months before Jesus and his disciples returned to Jerusalem for the final Passover.

While Jesus was in Jerusalem for the Feast of Dedication, the Jews seized the opportunity to surround him and ask their question, "How long will you keep us in suspense? If you are the Christ, tell us plainly." The question seems unnecessary to us. Jesus had spoken clearly at the Feast of Booths. He had claimed to be sent from God above and even claimed, "Before Abraham was, I am" (John 8:58). They had picked up stones to kill him, but Jesus had slipped away. His time had not yet come. The exchanges between Jesus and the Pharisees left no doubt who Jesus claimed to be, but the Pharisees did not believe. The disciples of Jesus understood he was the Messiah, and many who heard him also believed. Jesus concluded his comments two months earlier at the Feast of Booths by claiming to be the Good Shepherd who knew his sheep and would lay down his life for the sheep. He claimed that he had received his mission from his Father (John 10:17-18). We have grown to treasure his words, but he had left Jerusalem divided over who he was. That's the reason for this question now on his return.

Jesus returned to the theme of the Good Shepherd and asserted once again that he had come on the mission his Father above had given him. "I told you, and you do not believe," he said. The words about his sheep have combined in our minds with what he said at the earlier festival. They are wonderful, gracious assurances of his love for his sheep and a beautiful promise of eternal life. "My sheep hear my voice, and I know them, and they follow me. I give them eternal life, and they will never perish, and no one will snatch them out of my hand."

What comfort those words give us in the face of life's trials. Consider part of that original audience—the Jews in Jerusalem who believed in him. One of his goals was to confirm their faith in him. Later they would face increasing opposition from the Pharisees and Jewish leaders. Those who followed Jesus already were threatened with expulsion from the synagogue (John 9:22). The believers in Jerusalem and those who followed him on his travels—including Peter, James, John, and the others—would be intimidated, bullied, and imprisoned even after Pentecost. But Jesus promised that none of this could "snatch them out of the Father's hand"—another lesson for his disciples. These words of Jesus also apply to us as we face opposition, intimidation, bullying, and threats because we are followers of Jesus.

In addition, Jesus asserted that he gives eternal life to his sheep. Since the beginning of his ministry, he had made the same promise. From his early meeting with Nicodemus in the night (John 3:1-6) to his feeding of the five thousand (John 6:1-14) and now again, Jesus promised eternal life to those who believe in him. Impossible, the Jews in Jerusalem thought, and they picked up stones to kill him. Yes, it was impossible if Jesus were only a human like them. But he was the one "the Father consecrated and sent into the world." He had the power and authority to make such a promise. But that only incensed them again. They tried to seize him once more, but Jesus escaped. Even that escape was a witness of his power, but neither his words nor his escape mattered to them. They would continue to look for a way to kill him. They would succeed, but not yet and only when the time came that Jesus had planned for—Passover, only a few months away.

PRAYER: Lord Jesus, you are my powerful Shepherd who promises me eternal life. I rejoice at your promise and the hope I have because of it. Yet many have discarded your promise as an impossible dream. Others openly mock and ridicule you. As you have promised, keep me as one of your sheep so that I may listen to you, find protection in your power, and finally, receive eternal life. Amen.

50

Return to Perea

[Jesus] went away again across the Jordan to the place where John had been baptizing at first, and there he remained. And many came to him. And they said, "John did no sign, but everything that John said about this man was true." And many believed in him there. (John 10:40-42)

The disciples had gone with Jesus to Jerusalem twice in the past two and a half months. Twice they had witnessed the opposition in Jerusalem. Their memory of the Pharisees with stones in their hands created a vivid reminder and was tinged with fear for Jesus and themselves. But they were with Jesus, not some powerless teacher. They knew he was more than just a teacher and felt protected in his company. Yet they returned to Perea with vivid memories of what had happened at both festivals.

With Jerusalem once again in the rearview mirror, they found a more comfortable and familiar atmosphere—a quiet place to listen, watch, and learn. Many people came to see and hear Jesus. It was not Galilee, but it certainly was not Jerusalem either. John tells us that across the Jordan, "many believed in him there." With the exception of a couple of journeys out of Perea, Jesus and the disciples would remain there for the next three months. Jesus would use the time to continue to teach his disciples and bring others to faith in him.

The events of these three months are not easy to place in order. Jesus came here after the Feast of Booths and then again after the Feast of Dedication. Some suggest that here in Perea, Jesus repeated many of the lessons he had already taught earlier in his ministry. That is quite possible because he had not spent a great deal of time in Perea: This audience was new. Whatever happened in Perea, the gospels don't tell us in a neat chronology.

We are children of the Greeks and Romans in our thinking. They liked sequence, chronology, and logical order. The Jews were different. I once had someone describe the difference between the Greek mind and the Hebrew mind. He said the Greek or Western mind likes to put things in order like pearls on a string. The Hebrew mind puts those same pearls in a bag; you have to choose how they fit together. We need to keep that in mind when we read the Scriptures. Paul is more Greek-minded, but the gospels are often more Hebrew-minded.

We do have some clues about the chronology. For example, John identifies the festivals and helps us put the events in order. Sometimes the other gospel writers give us clues too, but when they write that Jesus went up to Jerusalem, we may question when that happened. For which Passover or which festival did Jesus go to Jerusalem? Even if the events recorded for us by the gospels are out of order at times, the gospels are the record of eyewitnesses and are reliable. That's what is important.

In addition, Jesus promised he would send the Holy Spirit to the disciples after he ascended and was gone from them. In the upper room he promised, "But the Helper, the Holy Spirit, whom the Father will send in my name, he will teach you all things and bring to your remembrance all that I have said to you" (John 14:26). We are not dealing with a powerless teacher whose words cannot be trusted. He is the one sent by the Father to teach us and proclaim the good news. That's what he had been doing since his baptism by John. As he said in Nazareth, he was anointed to proclaim the good news.

Here the apostle John records an interesting note. Jesus now returned "to the place where John had been baptizing at first," where God identified Jesus as his beloved Son in whom he was well pleased (Matthew 3:17). It's also where John pointed to Jesus and announced, "Behold, the Lamb of God" (John 1:29). In the company of John, Andrew heard it and shared the news with his brother Peter. Did the region bring back memories of those simpler, exciting days? The disciples had learned so much in the meantime but still had lessons to learn. In the past year, Jesus had been preparing them for the next chapter—the time when he would no longer be with them.

Jesus knew that his hour was coming—and soon. He had explained to his disciples that he would be handed over, that is, betrayed, into the hands of Jewish leaders, killed, but rise again. The disciples had resisted his words at first and then were perplexed by them when he repeated them. They would not understand what he meant until Jesus was betrayed by Judas and crucified by the Romans. When the stone was rolled away from the tomb on the third day, at first they were only afraid and hid behind locked doors. But Jesus would spend another 40 days assuring them and teaching what his life, death, and resurrection meant.

Everything was coming full circle. The one baptized by John here across the Jordan River would eventually step across the river and head to Jerusalem for one final trip. Jesus knew what was soon to happen. He was still his Father's well-loved and obedient Son. He would finish the mission given to him at the beginning.

Like those in Perea, Galilee, and Jerusalem, we believe in him and have believed in him. Those who heard him in Perea all those years ago concluded, "Everything that John said about this man was true." We have heard so much more and have the clarity of knowing Jesus died and rose again. All John said at the Jordan River in the beginning and all that the eyewitnesses have said about Jesus were true. The men in Jerusalem who stood with stones in their hands ready to kill Jesus could not change that. Those who oppose him now and question what the eyewitnesses tell us about him cannot change the truth either. Look, the Lamb of God who takes away the sin of the world.

PRAYER: Lord Jesus, always let me find a quiet place to learn your truth. Dispel any doubts about the words of the eyewitnesses or their reliability. You are the Lamb of God, recognized by Peter, James, John, Matthew, and others as the Savior of the world. Teach me always to treasure what you have done for me and every sinner. Amen.

51

Seventy-Two

After this the Lord appointed seventy-two others and sent them on ahead of him, two by two, into every town and place where he himself was about to go. And he said to them, "The harvest is plentiful, but the laborers are few. Therefore pray earnestly to the Lord of the harvest to send out laborers into his harvest. Go your way; behold, I am sending you out as lambs in the midst of wolves. The one who hears you hears me, and the one who rejects you rejects me, and the one who rejects me rejects him who sent me." The seventy-two returned with joy, saying, "Lord, even the demons are subject to us in your name!" And he said to them, "I saw Satan fall like lightning from heaven." In that same hour he rejoiced in the Holy Spirit and said, "I thank you, Father, Lord of heaven and earth, that you have hidden these things from the wise and understanding and revealed them to little children; yes, Father, for such was your gracious will. All things have been handed over to me by my Father, and no one knows who the Son is except the Father, or who the Father is except the Son and anyone to whom the Son chooses to reveal him." Then turning to the disciples he said privately, "Blessed are the eyes that see what you see! For I tell you that many prophets and kings desired to see what you see, and did not see it, and to hear what you hear, and did not hear it." (Luke 10:1-3,16-18,21-24)

Earlier in his ministry Jesus sent the 12 disciples (Matthew 10; Luke 9) to the villages of Galilee to proclaim the good news and heal the sick. Jesus told them that the harvest was plentiful. A lot had happened since then, and the harvest was still plentiful. When the harvest is plentiful and it is too much for the workers to handle, a farmer must hire more workers to send into the field. If he does not add workers, the crop will remain in the field.

When Jesus sent the Twelve, he intended to teach them through the experience. They gained a vision of the work that Jesus was doing—teaching the good news. They participated in that work. That was a part of the lesson too. They had listened and watched Jesus teach and heal. Now they were given the privilege of sharing the message of salvation and healing the sick.

Although they didn't know it yet, that was what they would do the rest of their lives. Jesus would ascend into heaven after his suffering, death, and resurrection and then turn the task of proclaiming the good news completely over to them. That was always part of the mission Jesus' heavenly Father had given him: to proclaim the good news; to train others to proclaim it; and to suffer, die, and rise again so that there actually was good news to tell.

Jesus humbled himself and became a servant—a human—to be obedient to death, as Paul wrote, "even death on a cross" (Philippians 2:8). His miracles demonstrated and validated his mission and message, but he was one human who substituted himself for all humans and paid the penalty for all human sins. As one human, he chose to assume all the limitations of humans. He walked, talked, ate, and grew tired. As that servant, he could not be and proclaim the good news everywhere. Another part of his mission was to gather some and send them out into the villages and expand his reach with the good news. The training of these 12 men, including their journey to the villages, was a privilege. What an experience! What a confidence builder!

But the work did not fall on only their shoulders. Jesus encouraged the Twelve. "The harvest is plentiful, but the laborers are few; therefore pray earnestly to the Lord of the harvest to send out laborers into his harvest" (Matthew 9:37-38). Sometime later—either in Galilee, Judea, or Perea—Jesus expanded the labor force. Their prayers and his had brought 72 new faces to share the work. Jesus sent them out with very similar instructions. They were to go out as lambs among wolves, but Jesus assured them, "The one who hears you hears me, and the one who rejects you rejects me, and the one who rejects me rejects him who sent me." They were to proclaim, "The kingdom of God has come near to you" (Luke 10:9). He encouraged these men too, just as he had the Twelve: "Therefore pray earnestly to the Lord of the harvest to send out laborers into his harvest."

These 72 workers had the same opportunity to learn the lessons needed to share the gospel after Jesus ascended. They too were thrilled with the experience and returned with joy. Their joy of proclaiming the gospel brought Jesus joy. He saw their success vividly and rejoiced, "I saw Satan fall like lightning from heaven." The proclamation of the gospel strikes a blow against Satan's efforts to bring trouble, persecution, sorrow, and misery into the world. The joy in the heart of Jesus burst into praise that his heavenly Father had revealed the truth to these 72 and all those who believed in him. They were little children trusting simply in Jesus.

The disciples had seen so much. They saw what many prophets and kings wanted to see but did not. They heard the words of God from Jesus himself—what Abraham, Isaac, and Jacob had longed to hear. What a privilege these 72 had. We also have a privilege. We have heard and seen what they did. We were not there to see all these events with our own eyes, but the eyewitness accounts of the apostles are recorded for us. What a blessing we have. The harvest is still plentiful, and the laborers are still few. Our task is the same—to share the gospel we have and pray for workers to share it.

PRAYER: Lord Jesus, I have heard and trusted your words. By the power of the Holy Spirit, those words have made me a disciple. You have sent me out as a lamb among wolves with the assurance that whoever rejects me rejects you. Yet you have encouraged me with your promise that whoever listens to me listens to you. Strengthen me as your messenger, and send more laborers into the harvest to reach more than I can. For the sake of your kingdom. Amen.

52

Neighbors

Behold, a lawyer stood up to put him to the test, saying, "Teacher, what shall I do to inherit eternal life?" He said to him, "What is written in the Law? How do you read it?" And he answered, "You shall love the Lord your God with all your heart and with all your soul and with all your strength and with all your mind, and your neighbor as yourself." And he said to him, "You have answered correctly; do this, and you will live." But he, desiring to justify himself, said to Jesus, "And who is my neighbor?" Jesus replied, "A man was going down from Jerusalem to Jericho, and he fell among robbers, who stripped him and beat him and departed, leaving him half dead. Now by chance a priest was going down that road, and when he saw him he passed by on the other side. So likewise a Levite, when he came to the place and saw him, passed by on the other side. But a Samaritan, as he journeyed, came to where he was, and when he saw him, he had compassion. He went to him and bound up his wounds, pouring on oil and wine. Then he set him on his own animal and brought him to an inn and took care of him. And the next day he took out two denarii and gave them to the innkeeper, saying, 'Take care of him, and whatever more you spend, I will repay you when I come back.' Which of these three, do you think, proved to be a neighbor to the man who fell among the robbers?" He said, "The one who showed him mercy." And Jesus said to him, "You go, and do likewise." (Luke 10:25-37)

This incident sounds familiar. Mark records a similar question from a rich young man (Mark 10:17-27). The man in this devotion is a lawyer, an expert in the law. Both evangelists could be describing the same person. The expert in the law could be young and rich as well. But one asks a sincere question from a troubled heart and the other asks a question to "put [Jesus] to the test." While the question is similar, the exchanges between Jesus and the two men are also quite different. We do not know just where this event took place. But no matter where it happened, the parable of the good Samaritan is a gem of the Savior's teaching and familiar to almost everyone, even those who do not share our Christian faith.

Jesus must have been asked this question about eternal life many times as he taught the people. He had also fielded questions about which of the commandments was most important. Some asked these questions to make Jesus look bad when he answered. Jesus always answered and, in some cases, answered so clearly and thoroughly that those who tested him didn't dare ask any additional questions. But this man boldly asked, "Teacher, what shall I do to inherit eternal life?"

The lawyer was steeped in the law. He believed that eternal life was the reward for what one did. That natural idea comes to every human heart. At the funerals of many, we hear of the departed and the good they have done. It's a popular notion that the good go to heaven and the bad do not. Jesus explored that idea with this expert. "What is written in the Law?" he asked. As an expert in the law, the man quickly responded, reciting two important principles: love God and love your neighbor.

Jesus said, "Do this; and you will live." Yes. Love God "with all your heart and with all your soul and with all your mind and with all your strength" (Mark 12:30). If the lawyer could do that he would live, but could he do it? Can anyone? He may have felt confident in his love for God, but he would encounter his failure if he compared his thoughts, words, and actions with the "all" of the law. Then what about "love . . . your neighbor as yourself"? Could he put himself on an equal footing with his neighbor? The human heart naturally loves others only after we have loved ourselves and first take care of our wants. Love others as yourself? "Do this; and you will live." Yes, do it as God says. Fulfill the law completely and fully and you can live. But we cannot "do this," so we cannot live.

Still thinking that he could do what the law required, the lawyer wanted to know who his neighbor was. Then Jesus destroys the man's pretensions with the parable of the good Samaritan. A man in trouble needed help, but both priest and Levite passed by without lending aid. Did Jesus' choice of these two Jewish religious examples subtly include the lawyer? To complete the challenge, Jesus introduced a Samaritan. To the Jews—and to this expert in the Jewish Scriptures—the Samaritan was an inferior person. He was not one of their kind. The Jews did not even travel through Samaria on their way from Galilee to the festivals in Jerusalem. Yet this inferior man offered aid and not just minimal aid. He bandaged the man's wounds, brought him to an inn, took care of him, and promised to pay for his recovery.

The lesson should have been complete. Jesus asked who in the parable was the neighbor. There was only one answer, but the lawyer could not even say, "The Samaritan." Instead, he said, "The one who showed him mercy." "Go, and do likewise," Jesus answered. That must have stung the lawyer's prejudices and his concepts of loving others. The point was that the law convicts and cannot help anyone "to inherit eternal life." To inherit, one had to be a son or daughter. But no one is a son or daughter because of his or her deeds. We become heirs of eternal life because Jesus has adopted us as his sons and daughters. He has cleansed us of all our sins. By faith in him we are sons and daughters who inherit eternal life.

The lesson to love others was important for the disciples after Jesus ascended. They learned it, but they had difficulty with it at first. Later those outside the church noticed that the Christians helped others who had trouble but were not of their kind. The compassion and love of Christians of the early church caused many to pause and consider the message of the gospel. Then they were drawn to believe and become heirs of eternal life.

PRAYER: Lord Jesus, I can never be good enough to inherit eternal life by any actions of mine. Yet you have come here to win forgiveness and cleanse me so that I am your adopted child and heir of eternal life. Help me overcome my prejudices and selfishness so that I love all others. When I am tempted to withhold love, remind me of your undeserved love for me so that I love others. Amen.

53

A Stop at Bethany

Now as they went on their way, Jesus entered a village. And a woman named Martha welcomed him into her house. And she had a sister called Mary, who sat at the Lord's feet and listened to his teaching. But Martha was distracted with much serving. And she went up to him and said, "Lord, do you not care that my sister has left me to serve alone? Tell her then to help me." But the Lord answered her, "Martha, Martha, you are anxious and troubled about many things, but one thing is necessary. Mary has chosen the good portion, which will not be taken away from her." (Luke 10:38-42)

Luke places this story after Jesus told the parable of the good Samaritan. Like many of these incidents, we can't be sure where they fit chronologically, but this visit to Bethany at the end of Jesus' public ministry is important. It may have occurred earlier, but the importance of Bethany in the last week of the Savior's life gives us at least something to think about. Bethany was only a short distance from Jerusalem and therefore an important location for Passion Week. Jesus arrived in Bethany six days before the Passover (John 12:1). The next day, Palm Sunday, Jesus entered Jerusalem and then returned to Bethany (Matthew 21:17). On Monday morning he returned to Jerusalem and taught in the temple. In the evening he went out of the city to the Mount of Olives. It was the place where Judas and the mob later found him Thursday night.

Jesus had close ties to Bethany and the home of Mary, Martha, and Lazarus. He was a welcome guest in the house. Martha was instrumental in making him welcome and providing the food necessary for the guests, including the disciples. What a privilege it was for them all to have Jesus with them. Perhaps this visit was a bit unexpected since

Martha busied herself with preparations. Jesus gathered his disciples in the house or just outside the house and took the opportunity to teach. Mary, Martha's sister, chose to duck out of the preparations and sit with the others to listen to Jesus.

Preparing for the visit was a big task, and Martha soon was overwhelmed. She was looking for help. She wanted all to be perfect for this visit by Jesus and his disciples. Mary was not with Martha as she worked hard to be hospitable to her guests. She grew resentful and peevish. Her sister was sitting and listening to Jesus instead of collecting food and wielding a knife. Tension grew until she broke in on Jesus to complain, "Lord, do you not care that my sister has left me to serve alone? Tell her then to help me."

When we think of the New Testament Scriptures, we ought never think of them as the creation of some philosophical scribe who had no contact with real events. The details of this short event testify to its truth. This human encounter with real people is not a staged and sterile encounter told for the sake of making a point. If you have a brother or sister, you know how naturally Martha's feelings and words came. Luke has talked with these two women (Luke 1:1-4) and captured their story carefully.

There's a point to the story, of course, and Jesus makes that point: "Martha, Martha, you are anxious and troubled about many things, but one thing is necessary. Mary has chosen the good portion, which will not be taken away from her." Listening to Jesus is better than scurrying around making preparations for the guests.

Listening to Jesus was the reason crowds flocked to Jesus wherever he went. Some opposed his words, but many wanted to hear what he said. Once, Jesus entered a boat on the Sea of Galilee to address the crowd because they were "pressing in on him to hear the word of God" (Luke 5:1). Later, Jesus addressed the crowd in Jerusalem in the temple during Passion Week. Mark wrote that "the great throng heard him gladly" (Mark 12:37). The words from heaven that Peter, James, and John heard at the transfiguration included the command "Listen to him" (Matthew 17:5). Mary did. Jesus would not reverse her decision, for she had chosen what was better.

Why listen to him? Why read the record of his words and deeds? Jesus had spent almost the entire Feast of Booths maintaining that his message was from above. He told the people from the beginning, "My time has not yet come, but your time is always here" (John 7:6). The Pharisees in Jerusalem rejected that claim, but many believed. The delight his words gave people was certainly because those words came from above. Their delight in hearing them increased because of the promises of God's love and God's blessing. Peter said it well: "Lord, to whom shall we go? You have the words of eternal life" (John 6:68).

Jesus was showing the disciples what the kingdom of heaven was all about. It was about the Word. It was sowing the seed of the Word as he taught in the parable of the sower. Mary's heart was the fertile soil in which the seed would take root and grow. The seed had already spouted in Martha's heart, and it also had taken root and grown, but she made a different choice. Listening to the Word was better than scurrying about with preparations, even if those preparations were for the Lord of life. We too are reminded to take time to sit and listen to Jesus. He speaks to us in the Scriptures. We gather together to hear his message in our worship, and we can also find time each day to pause and take a break from our daily tasks to read his Word and listen.

PRAYER: Lord Jesus, your Word is truth. You have communicated all I need to know about forgiveness, eternal life, and salvation. When distractions take me away from your message, call me back and welcome me to take my place in the crowd that delights in your Word. Amen.

54

At the Pharisee's Table

One Sabbath, when [Jesus] went to dine at the house of a ruler of the Pharisees, they were watching him carefully. And behold, there was a man before him who had dropsy. And Jesus responded to the lawyers and Pharisees, saying, "Is it lawful to heal on the Sabbath, or not?" But they remained silent. Then he took him and healed him and sent him away. And he said to them, "Which of you, having a son or an ox that has fallen into a well on a Sabbath day, will not immediately pull him out?" And they could not reply to these things. Now he told a parable to those who were invited, when he noticed how they chose the places of honor, saying to them, "When you are invited by someone to a wedding feast, do not sit down in a place of honor, lest someone more distinguished than you be invited by him, and he who invited you both will come and say to you, 'Give your place to this person,' and then you will begin with shame to take the lowest place. But when you are invited, go and sit in the lowest place, so that when your host comes he may say to you, 'Friend, move up higher.' Then you will be honored in the presence of all who sit at table with you. For everyone who exalts himself will be humbled, and he who humbles himself will be exalted." (Luke 14:1-11)

Silence. I imagine that it was awkward. Jesus was invited to the house of a prominent Pharisee. Everyone knew that Jesus had many enemies among the Pharisees. They had been plotting his death for a long time. So the house would hold no warm welcome but only watchful stares. Yet he went.

What happened was what almost anyone would expect. It was the Sabbath, and they were looking for something Jesus did or said that would confirm their rejection of him and his message. It didn't take long: "There was a man before him who had dropsy." Was this staged just for Jesus? He had healed on the Sabbath before. Perhaps a trap was the reason for this gathering at the Pharisee's house. Would Jesus do what he had done before, or had he learned from the objection of other Pharisees? Would he do what they wanted and withhold his healing touch? Would he heal?

Jesus did not wait. He repeated the question many of them had on their minds: "Is it lawful to heal on the Sabbath, or not?" He knew what they were trying to do. Their silence revealed their embarrassment at what they were trying to do—test Jesus using this poor man's suffering from abnormal swelling. They showed no compassion for that man or his family. He was just a prop in a test case, not even a man with feelings and thoughts. They had robbed him of his privacy, his individuality, and his dignity.

The touch of Jesus bridged the cruel effort. He was compassionate. Jesus healed him and then sent him on his way, giving him a blessed escape and a dignified return to his own life. The suddenness of Jesus' healing needed no further commentary. The unpleasant episode was over. The Pharisees had nothing to say.

But Jesus added a short comment: The Pharisees would not treat their own children or even their own animals the way they treated this man. Wouldn't they offer help if they could? And if they could not heal this man, could they not at least ask Jesus to help him in their presence? Their continued silence was an embarrassing confession of their attitudes toward Jesus, this man, and the law of the Sabbath.

But there was more. The house may have been silent, but the guests came looking for the seat of honor. This was the house of a prominent Pharisee who was respected and probably powerful. Those who were invited sought to curry favor not only with the host but also with the other guests. Being invited was an honor itself, but a place of honor at the table would impress everyone who attended. Humility stood outside, barred from entering. Concern for others disappeared when the man who was healed left.

The brief parable that Jesus taught was a crushing indictment of the guests' pride and self-importance. Once you hear it, you don't forget it unless you are so wrapped up in your own self-importance that you think it applies only to others. Jesus left no doubt about the lesson. "For everyone who exalts himself will be humbled, and he who humbles himself will be exalted." Just when you think you are important, there's always someone else who is really important—more important than you.

What makes this parable so striking is that it was Jesus speaking. He was an honored guest at the Pharisee's table, but he was more important than the host or any of his guests would admit. He was the Son of God whose Father had sent him from heaven on a mission to suffer, die, and rise again for all humanity. Yet he sat at that table to eat with others. There was no one more important than he, but he humbly came at the request of a Pharisee, even a prominent one, who surely knew of the plot against the Messiah and perhaps had even planned it.

In this context, the parable of Jesus was brutal to the self-importance of the Pharisees. But the lesson is also valuable for us. It's a lesson in humility for everyone, and one we should not neglect in our dealings with others. It's a lesson the disciples had difficulty with when they argued over who was the greatest. The apostle Paul applied the Lord's concerns to everyday Christians: "Do nothing from selfish ambition or conceit, but in humility count others more significant than yourselves" (Philippians 2:3). Considering how the Lord of heaven and earth humbled himself for us, we have not only his words but also a great example and motivation to humble ourselves.

PRAYER: Lord, so easily and so often I think I am so much better than others and seek opportunities to boast or to put others down. Forgive me for my conceit, self-promotion, and failure to treat others with honor, dignity, and respect. Because of your mercy and love for me as a lowly sinner, I have become your honored child by faith. Help me live as your child and in humility lest I allow my own pride to cause me and others to stumble. Amen.

55

Invitation

When one of those who reclined at table with [Jesus] heard these things, he said to him, "Blessed is everyone who will eat bread in the kingdom of God!" But he said to him, "A man once gave a great banquet and invited many. And at the time for the banquet he sent his servant to say to those who had been invited, 'Come, for everything is now ready.' But they all alike began to make excuses. The first said to him, 'I have bought a field, and I must go out and see it. Please have me excused.' And another said, 'I have bought five yoke of oxen, and I go to examine them. Please have me excused.' And another said, 'I have married a wife, and therefore I cannot come.' So the servant came and reported these things to his master. Then the master of the house became angry and said to his servant, 'Go out quickly to the streets and lanes of the city, and bring in the poor and crippled and blind and lame.' And the servant said, 'Sir, what you commanded has been done, and still there is room.' And the master said to the servant, 'Go out to the highways and hedges and compel people to come in, that my house may be filled. For I tell you, none of those men who were invited shall taste my banquet.'" (Luke 14:15-24)

We are still at the house of the prominent Pharisee. After Jesus chastised the Pharisees for their exalted opinion of themselves, one of those at the table finally spoke. "Blessed is everyone who will eat bread in the kingdom of God!" That comment not only opened the curtain of silence drawn by the Pharisees, but it also allowed Jesus to shift the focus once more. The event had started with the Pharisees carefully and silently watching whether Jesus would heal on the Sabbath. Then attention had shifted to the positions of honor the Pharisees sought for themselves.

Now the remark of one of the guests at this meal changed the focus again. Jesus turned the focus to the feast in the kingdom of God and issued an invitation with a serious warning to any who offered excuses not to attend. Those seated at the meal in the Pharisee's house easily understood what Jesus was saying about a great banquet prepared by a certain man: a servant of the Pharisee had come to their doors to invite them. All those present had accepted the invitation; no excuses had been offered.

Jesus does not give the meaning of this parable. It is self-evident. Jesus used the idea of a banquet again and altered it slightly, but the meaning remained clear. A certain man had prepared the banquet. He had graciously decided to host the banquet and made all the preparations. The invited guests did nothing to add to his preparations. It was all done. All that remained was to issue the invitation and wait for his guests to arrive.

So the Lord God had prepared the feast in the kingdom of God. He graciously prepared all things. Then the Lord sent his servant, the Anointed One, the Messiah, to issue the invitation to the chosen people. As Jesus said in Nazareth, he was "anointed . . . to proclaim good news" (Luke 4:18). The invitation was sent out to the people of Israel, who knew he was coming because the prophets had foretold his coming. What these Pharisees and others did not know yet was that the Messiah, or the Christ, would not only issue the invitation, but he would also complete the preparations by his suffering, death, and resurrection. He would announce from the cross, "It is finished" (John 19:30).

Then came the reactions to the invitation. Excuses. Excuses. They are politely offered and make sense: I just bought a field, I just bought oxen, or I just got married. They are reasonable excuses; nevertheless, they are refusals to come to the banquet. The owner of the house was angry. He had graciously prepared a great banquet, but those invited had more important things to do than go to the banquet. The owner sent his servant to go and invite the poor, crippled, blind, and lame. The banquet hall was still not full, so the servant was sent to the roads and country lanes to fill the hall with guests. Then the warning, "For I tell you, none of those men who were invited shall taste my banquet."

Jesus had been issuing the invitation of his heavenly Father his entire ministry. Some refused to believe. Others, like the Pharisees, vigorously opposed Jesus. But Jesus had taken his message of good news to Galilee, Decapolis, and Perea. The lame, the blind, the poor, and the crippled eagerly accepted him. They also felt his healing power. When Jesus adapted and retold the banquet parable in Jerusalem during Passion Week, the violent opposition grew (Matthew 22). He was issuing an invitation seeking the repentance of those who oppose him, warning them that to refuse the invitation means that they will be excluded from the feast in the kingdom of God.

The application of the parable rings true as the gospel was spread after Jesus ascended. Consider the missionary journeys of Paul. He went to the synagogues first to proclaim the gospel, but when the Jews there refused and opposed the good news, he went to the Gentiles and many gladly believed.

The application also applies to our world. As disciples of Jesus, we issue his invitation just as his disciples did long ago. Often, we experience polite excuses and refusals. Family, business, work, and a host of other excuses result in refusal to heed the invitation. Then when some complain that God is cruel when he closes the door of heaven on them, the truth is that he doesn't shut the door as much as he sadly watches them go their own way. They make excuses and continue making excuses to the very end. What is he to do with those who do not wish to attend the banquet he has prepared for all humanity? The last words of this parable apply to so many: "I tell you, none of those men who were invited shall taste my banquet."

PRAYER: Lord Almighty, you have prepared a great banquet for all humanity. You sent your Son to finish the preparations with his death on the cross and invited all humanity to come and believe in him. I praise you for your invitation in the gospel that has created faith in me. Now I have a place at your banquet table. Lord, keep me constant in faith so that I may finally take the place you have prepared for me. Amen.

56

Count the Cost

Now great crowds accompanied him, and he turned and said to them, "If anyone comes to me and does not hate his own father and mother and wife and children and brothers and sisters, yes, and even his own life, he cannot be my disciple. Whoever does not bear his own cross and come after me cannot be my disciple. For which of you, desiring to build a tower, does not first sit down and count the cost, whether he has enough to complete it? Otherwise, when he has laid a foundation and is not able to finish, all who see it begin to mock him, saying, 'This man began to build and was not able to finish.' So therefore, any one of you who does not renounce all that he has cannot be my disciple. Salt is good, but if salt has lost its taste, how shall its saltiness be restored? It is of no use either for the soil or for the manure pile. It is thrown away. He who has ears to hear, let him hear." (Luke 14:25-30,33-35)

In spite of the opposition in Jerusalem, John notes, "As he was saying these things, many believed in him" (John 8:30). At the end of what Jesus said about the Good Shepherd and the sheep at the Feast of Booths, people were divided between those who thought Jesus was demon-possessed and those who thought differently. "Many of them said, 'He has a demon, and is insane; why listen to him?' Others said, 'These are not the words of one who is oppressed by a demon. Can a demon open the eyes of the blind?'" (John 10:20-21). About two months later at the end of the Feast of Dedication, Jesus left Jerusalem and crossed back into Perea.

"And many came to him" (John 10:41). Many people came to know and treasure Jesus. But did they understand what it meant to follow Jesus? There was opposition from Jerusalem—serious opposition focused on destroying Jesus and those who followed him. A warning was in place—a dose of reality. Just a few months later, perhaps only a few weeks, Jesus would head to Jerusalem on his final pilgrimage. He knew what was ahead. The crowds did not. What they witnessed in Jerusalem would shatter many of their ideas about following Jesus.

They needed to hear a lesson. Jesus turned to the crowds with some stern words about discipleship. The lesson was important. He said, "If anyone comes to me and does not hate his own father and mother and wife and children and brothers and sisters, yes, and even his own life, he cannot be my disciple." Examples of discipleship were everywhere. Peter, Andrew, James, and John had left behind their nets and businesses. Matthew gave up his career as a tax collector. Not all followers of Jesus had to give up such things, but all followers of Jesus would have to change priorities. As disciples of Jesus, they had willingly made a place in their lives for him, even if it was still necessary to care for family and business. Most of the people who followed Jesus had homes, families, and livelihoods. They were not to abandon those obligations. Yet disciples of Jesus knew what was important—of first importance. Jesus became the pearl of great price and the hidden treasure (Matthew 13:44-46). All else became secondary. Some among the Twelve and the 72 had responsibilities for family—"but whatever gain I had, I counted as loss for the sake of Christ. Indeed, I count everything as loss because of the surpassing worth of knowing Christ Jesus my Lord. For his sake I have suffered the loss of all things and count them as rubbish, in order that I may gain Christ and be found in him, not having a righteousness of my own that comes from the law, but that which comes through faith in Christ, the righteousness from God that depends on faith" (Philippians 3:7-9).

What did Jesus see ahead for those who followed him? Perhaps some of them remembered the opposition in Jerusalem, the stones and angry words. Were they ready to endure opposition and ridicule because of their allegiance to Jesus? What other hardships or crosses would they have to bear? Crosses awaited them in the days and years ahead. Every disciple of Jesus faces those things. Having Christ means having all the blessings only he can provide. Disciples of Jesus bear the crosses rather than abandon Jesus.

Priorities. Priorities. Priorities. Jesus first. If you build a tower, you would count the cost before you started. We know that Jesus has already built a mansion for us and has rooms for all believers (John 14:2-4). He made the full payment with his blood. We don't have to build the mansion again. He waits for us to move in. The cost of getting there is to continue as disciples of Jesus until he calls us home. Disciples live in a world of difficulty, opposition, pain, and uncertainty. But through every twist and turn, even every challenge to their faith, they stay the course knowing what lies ahead. Even death does not change our course. We remain his disciples and salt here in this world. Disciples find a place for Jesus at the top of their list of must-haves. Then they pursue whatever it takes to follow, listen, watch, support, and proclaim Jesus while they do the other things that they need to take care of.

Jesus provides a perfect example for us. He counted the cost of coming to earth to redeem us. He realized it would cost him opposition, the dusty roads of Palestine, the incessant crowds, and then pain and death. He remained faithful to his Father's will in order to achieve our salvation. He died only to rise again. Our mansion is ready for us.

PRAYER: Lord, I want to follow you wherever you lead me. At times, Lord, I am distracted by the things of this life. Help me keep you as the one thing needful. Give me the strength to rearrange my priorities so that you are always first in what I think, say, and do. When I am tempted to set aside your Word and sacrament because I don't have time or my family tugs at me and pulls me away, draw me back to your Word and sacrament so that I may listen with undivided attention and follow you through all the daily crosses I must bear on my journey to your great banquet. Amen.

57

Joy in Heaven

The tax collectors and sinners were all drawing near to hear him. And the Pharisees and the scribes grumbled, saying, "This man receives sinners and eats with them." So he told them this parable: "What man of you, having a hundred sheep, if he has lost one of them, does not leave the ninety-nine in the open country, and go after the one that is lost, until he finds it? And when he has found it, he lays it on his shoulders, rejoicing. And when he comes home, he calls together his friends and his neighbors, saying to them, 'Rejoice with me, for I have found my sheep that was lost.' Just so, I tell you, there will be more joy in heaven over one sinner who repents than over ninety-nine righteous persons who need no repentance. Or what woman, having ten silver coins, if she loses one coin, does not light a lamp and sweep the house and seek diligently until she finds it? And when she has found it, she calls together her friends and neighbors, saying, 'Rejoice with me, for I have found the coin that I had lost.' Just so, I tell you, there is joy before the angels of God over one sinner who repents." (Luke 15:1-10)

Luke arranged this section of his gospel in an interesting progression of thoughts. He took us to the Pharisee's house where Jesus told a group of opponents about the great banquet and invited them to come and believe. But he also warned them of what would happen if they made excuses and did not believe. Then he included an encouragement for believers to value him and all he has done as of first importance. Finally, Jesus related these lessons to the joy in heaven for all who heed the invitation, believe, and remain faithful. Joy fills heaven for all who repent and are no longer lost and without God's love and promises.

God's goal is finding the lost, not punishing the sinner. Peter learned that lesson. He wrote that the Lord "is patient toward [us,] not wishing that any should perish, but that all should reach repentance" (2 Peter 3:9). The joy in heaven underscores that lesson, one the disciples needed to learn for the years ahead.

Pentecost was a dramatic event that called the lost to repentance. Peter proclaimed, "Repent and be baptized every one of you in the name of Jesus Christ for the forgiveness of your sins" (Acts 2:38). The call to repentance—the invitation to come to the feast of the kingdom of God—went to the Pharisees and experts of the law as well as the pilgrims who had come to Jerusalem for the festival. God had not given up on seeking the lost. Later, when the disciples were arrested and in prison, an angel brought them out and told them, "Go and stand in the temple and speak to the people all the words of this Life" (Acts 5:20). In the face of persecution, the apostles were commanded to seek the lost through their witness and that of the growing Christian congregation. And there was joy in heaven over each person who turned to Jesus in faith. So they continued.

In the midst of their proclamation of the gospel, the disciples would experience the same opposition that Jesus had faced. The Pharisees and the teachers of the law muttered about Jesus. They opposed the believers after Jesus ascended. When some believers fled because of the persecution, they carried the gospel message with them and shared it with the lost. Rejoice! God wants all to be saved. Consider the missionary journeys of Paul. Luke became part of that missionary team that God sent into the Mediterranean world of the Roman Empire. God even chose this time—the fullness of time—to make the invitation easier to spread through the advantages of the Roman world.

At times the Roman Empire was not a welcome place for Christians. Yet Paul stood before Roman officials and issued the invitation to believe in Jesus. Read the last chapter of Acts and consider how God goes "after the one that is lost, until he finds it." The invitation has never been irresistible. In Jesus' day, when he was here, excuses kept people from believing. His presence did not cause opposition to disappear. Excuses persisted in the early church too. Yet there was joy in heaven at every sheep that was lifted onto the Shepherd's shoulder and carried home.

As we think about what happened so long ago, we may be disappointed that the same call to repentance does not achieve the same success. But God has not stopped doing what the woman did when she had lost a coin. She searched carefully to find it. God still searches for the lost. He found you. He found me. Through us and other Christians around the world, God invites the lost to the feast of the kingdom he has prepared in Christ. As in every other age, many make excuses because they have more important things to do or think about than the banquet of heaven. Yet God continues to use us and others to seek those who need to hear his invitation. The Bible remains the most widely purchased book in the world. God places the banquet of heaven before so many. Some despise it, oppose it, or persecute his messengers, but "there is joy before the angels of God over one sinner who repents."

These readings in Luke's gospel remind us of the importance of holding firm to the Lord's promises in the face of all crosses and also of sharing God's invitation. Those who make excuses will not find joy, peace, or eternal life. Nevertheless, the banquet is prepared and ready for all. The joy of those who accept God's invitation fills heaven as well as the hearts of believers here and now.

PRAYER: Lord, you have found me, a lost and condemned creature. By your grace, someone has shared with me your invitation to the banquet in heaven, and I believe in Jesus who has prepared my place there. As your disciple, help me to keep you first in my thoughts and life. May the joy in heaven that came when you found me encourage me to share the gospel with others in whatever way I can so that heaven may rejoice in more sinners who repent. Amen.

58

My Son

[Jesus] said, "There was a man who had two sons. And the younger of them said to his father, 'Father, give me the share of property that is coming to me.' And he divided his property between them. Not many days later, the younger son gathered all he had and took a journey into a far country, and there he squandered his property in reckless living. And when he had spent everything, a severe famine arose in that country, and he began to be in need. So he went and hired himself out to one of the citizens of that country, who sent him into his fields to feed pigs. And he was longing to be fed with the pods that the pigs ate, and no one gave him anything. But when he came to himself, he said, 'How many of my father's hired servants have more than enough bread, but I perish here with hunger! I will arise and go to my father, and I will say to him, "Father, I have sinned against heaven and before you. I am no longer worthy to be called your son. Treat me as one of your hired servants."' And he arose and came to his father. But while he was still a long way off, his father saw him and felt compassion, and ran and embraced him and kissed him. And the son said to him, 'Father, I have sinned against heaven and before you. I am no longer worthy to be called your son.' But the father said to his servants, 'Bring quickly the best robe, and put it on him, and put a ring on his hand, and shoes on his feet. And bring the fattened calf and kill it, and let us eat and celebrate. For this my son was dead, and is alive again; he was lost, and is found.' And they began to celebrate." (Luke 15:11-24)

Jesus was an excellent teacher. Think of the parables he taught and the images those parables have left in the minds of those who heard him. Think of the images we have in our minds not just from the parables but also from his graphic illustrations. The Good Shepherd, the good Samaritan, the banquet parables, the sower, and the pearl of great price easily bring images. Many of us recall the lessons they taught. The parables came as Jesus faced opposition from those who wanted to kill him. No one was ever like him. We say that first for what he accomplished on the cross, but we can also say that for the way he taught his disciples and us.

Luke spent time talking with eyewitnesses of the ministry of Jesus. No doubt he talked with the 11 disciples and others who had heard and seen Jesus. The teaching of Jesus had made a deep impression on them and, in turn, their accounts made a deep impression on Luke. I don't know whether he took notes during his interviews or wrote them out and kept them somewhere until he was ready to write the entire gospel. Then he may have selected what to write, and the Holy Spirit blessed his interview process and his choices. According to the promise of Jesus, the Holy Spirit brought all these memories to Luke's mind and guided him—inspired him to put down on his manuscript the truth of these parables, other sayings, and what Jesus did. No wonder all the gospels spend a great deal of time telling us what happened during the last Passover week, but they also give us some remarkable other truths to treasure.

This is one of them. The parable gives us vivid, concrete images that we remember easily. In the plots of literature, the basic stories reappear often with, of course, variations of their meanings. For us, the meaning speaks again of the goodness of our heavenly Father receiving a wayward sinner back into his loving care. The joy in heaven over one sinner who repents is reinforced by the father's welcome of his prodigal son. What joy to see his lost son return!

Certainly, in this parable the idea of being lost includes important details. The son was dissatisfied with his life in the care of his father. He abandoned his father, took his inheritance, and "squandered his property in reckless living." Then the story turns to the son hitting rock bottom. He recognizes the foolishness of what he has done and wants to eat even the pods for the pigs—a significant bottom for any Jew and a detail added by the master to engage his audience. The son had his catharsis and resolved to return humbly to his father to seek only a job.

We know of such events from our own experiences. A son or daughter leaves, sometimes in anger and bitterness. Sometimes the ending is a happy one as in the parable Jesus told—the return and the joy that goes with it. But at other times the ending may not be so happy. "Reckless living" takes on new meaning in our drug-infested world, and young women and men die pathetically without a reunion with family and, more importantly, with God.

We also may know these events from personal experience. We may have abandoned our heavenly Father, perhaps for a long time. We may not pursue "reckless living," but we seek life without him and his Son, Jesus. We may offer excuses to avoid his truth and love because we think something else is more important or his message is too confining. We become delinquent children of God. Our story may not involve a long time away from God. Instead, we may turn daily from our Father's ways and his love when we seek to do our own thing.

This parable is about repentance and the stalwart, faithful, unending love of our heavenly Father for sinners like us. He has given us forgiveness and a place at his banquet. When we sometimes abandon what he has given us in Christ, he seeks us out, perhaps painfully, by letting us find the error of our ways. Then he stands ready to embrace us with his love when we return.

PRAYER: Lord Jesus, thank you for telling the parable of the prodigal son. It reminds me of your deep love for me and all people. When I seek to go my own way and abandon you and my heavenly Father, I pray that you do not abandon me. Call me back to your love. Help me turn away from the path that leads away from you so that I will again seek your love and forgiveness. Then embrace me with your love and give me peace and joy again. Amen.

59

Listen to His Word

"There was a rich man who was clothed in purple and fine linen and who feasted sumptuously every day. And at his gate was laid a poor man named Lazarus, covered with sores, who desired to be fed with what fell from the rich man's table. Moreover, even the dogs came and licked his sores. The poor man died and was carried by the angels to Abraham's side. The rich man also died and was buried, and in Hades, being in torment, he lifted up his eyes and saw Abraham far off and Lazarus at his side. And he called out, 'Father Abraham, have mercy on me, and send Lazarus to dip the end of his finger in water and cool my tongue, for I am in anguish in this flame.' But Abraham said, 'Child, remember that you in your lifetime received your good things, and Lazarus in like manner bad things; but now he is comforted here, and you are in anguish. And besides all this, between us and you a great chasm has been fixed, in order that those who would pass from here to you may not be able, and none may cross from there to us.' And he said, 'Then I beg you, father, to send him to my father's house—for I have five brothers—so that he may warn them, lest they also come into this place of torment.' But Abraham said, 'They have Moses and the Prophets; let them hear them.' And he said, 'No, father Abraham, but if someone goes to them from the dead, they will repent.' He said to him, 'If they do not hear Moses and the Prophets, neither will they be convinced if someone should rise from the dead.'" (Luke 16:19-31)

Often Jesus told parables when facing a mixed crowd of believers, the curious, and the hard-core opponents. He spoke parables "to fulfill what was spoken by the prophet: 'I will open my mouth in parables, I will utter what has been hidden since the foundation of the world'"

(Matthew 13:35, quoting Psalm 78:2). The hidden has always been the gospel. The Holy Spirit had to unravel it to make it understandable. That had already happened. Jesus told the disciples, "To you has been given the secret of the kingdom of God" (Mark 4:11). They understood God's grace in sending Jesus into the world, and they came to him and asked their questions. He readily explained.

On the other hand, the curious would return to listen again and to learn more. The opponents would reject whatever he said, however he said it. Parables were an open door inviting believers and the curious to enter and explore while frustrating the opponents and allowing Jesus to continue teaching the faithful and deepening their understanding. The gospel was and is a hidden mystery and foolish to the unbeliever but is the wisdom of God to the believer (1 Corinthians 1:18-19).

The rich man in this parable had no time for Moses and the prophets. He was wealthy. He had set his priorities on business, wealth, and luxury. He made excuses not to pay attention to the Scriptures. If he lived in Jerusalem, the temple was a focal point and the city was filled regularly with pilgrims attending the festivals. He did not pay attention. His five brothers had done the same.

The other man in the parable was a beggar named Lazarus. His situation, from a human perspective, was pathetic. He was the opposite of the rich man: eating scraps and finding relief in the licks of dogs. The difference extended to his attitude toward God. He was the one who was invited to the feast of the kingdom and who longed to be welcomed there.

Both men died, and the difference was clear but reversed after death. Lazarus was at peace in heaven, free from all earthly troubles. He had a place at the feast in the kingdom of God. The rich man had made his excuses in life and now could not "taste [Jesus'] banquet" (Luke 14:24).

Not only was the rich man excluded from the banquet, but he was also in torment—a torment that could not be changed or relieved even by a drop of water. Lazarus was with Abraham and was "comforted." Between the two was a barrier—a great chasm—that prevented anyone from either place crossing to the other side. The rich man soon abandoned any hope for himself but asked that his brothers be warned. He asked that Lazarus be returned from the dead to warn his brothers.

Jesus gave the answer in the parable of the great banquet (Luke 14:15-24). The answer deserves our attention. First, God's invitation to attend the banquet is part of his revelation through Moses and the prophets. The rich man had chosen not to heed the invitation. He had more important things in this life. God, on the other hand, has made the Scriptures part of his effort to seek and save the lost. There would be no special revelation for the man's brothers who remained alive. They had their own choices to make.

Second, in the parable Abraham said, "If they do not hear Moses and the Prophets, neither will they be convinced if someone should rise from the dead." Jesus had performed miracle after miracle, but his opponents did not believe even those miracles. If it had not already happened, it would when Jesus called back to life a man named Lazarus in Bethany. Instead of believing, the Pharisees grew more opposed than ever to Jesus and energized their plans to kill him.

Then in just a few weeks, Jesus himself would be killed but would rise from the dead. Yet the Pharisees and others remained opposed to all that Jesus said and did. The words at the end of this parable remain true even today. Those opposed to Jesus and his message refuse to believe the invitation of the Scriptures. The Scriptures include the eyewitnesses who saw and heard Jesus after he rose from the dead. Sadly, many continue to refuse the invitation of the Lord even though Jesus has risen.

PRAYER: By the power of the Holy Spirit, I have heard and believe your invitation to the banquet of heaven. While so many others continue to give your Word little attention and discount it as foolishness, help me to remain faithful. Keep me reading, studying, and meditating on your Word as my only source of your grace—my lifeline to grace and glory. Lord, give me the opportunity to share the invitation with others even if they continue to make excuses not to listen. Amen.

60

Return to Jerusalem

Jesus therefore no longer walked openly among the Jews, but went from there to the region near the wilderness, to a town called Ephraim, and there he stayed with the disciples. Now the Passover of the Jews was at hand, and many went up from the country to Jerusalem before the Passover to purify themselves. (John 11:54-55)

Taking the twelve, he said to them, "See, we are going up to Jerusalem, and everything that is written about the Son of Man by the prophets will be accomplished. For he will be delivered over to the Gentiles and will be mocked and shamefully treated and spit upon. And after flogging him, they will kill him, and on the third day he will rise." But they understood none of these things. This saying was hidden from them, and they did not grasp what was said. (Luke 18:31-34)

The ministry of Jesus in Perea was interrupted by a message from Mary and Martha in Bethany (John 11). They sent word that their brother Lazarus was sick and asked Jesus to come. He waited two days. Then he told his disciples, "Let us go to Judea again" (John 11:7). The disciples remembered the last visits to Judea. They objected, "Rabbi, the Jews were just now seeking to stone you, and are you going there again?" (John 11:8).

Jesus told the disciples, "Our friend Lazarus has fallen asleep, but I go to awaken him" (John 11:11). When they did not understand, he told them that Lazarus had died and explained, "For your sake I am glad that I was not there, so that you may believe. But let us go to him" (John 11:15). The disciples obediently followed, but not before Thomas encouraged the others, "Let us also go, that we may die with him" (John 11:16).

What happened in Bethany was an astonishing miracle. After Lazarus had been dead for four days, Jesus simply called him from his tomb. The sorrow of Mary and Martha eased with the words of comfort of Jesus. He told them, "I am the resurrection and the life. Whoever believes in me, though he die, yet shall he live, and everyone who lives and believes in me shall never die" (John 11:25-26). Those were more than comforting words from a heart wishing to offer hope. Jesus demonstrated the truth of those words by calling to their brother in the tomb, "Lazarus, come out" (John 11:43). And he did.

The miracle was reported to the Pharisees, and they called a special meeting of the Sanhedrin. The crowd in Jerusalem was frustrated with the miracle in Bethany. They were afraid that Jesus would grow so popular that "everyone will believe in him, and the Romans will come and take away both [their] place and [their] nation" (John 11:48). The high priest, Caiaphas, advised that one man should die for the people so that the whole nation would not perish. It was advice born of political necessity. Kill Jesus so the Romans would not change their policy and adopt another that might destroy their advantages as Jews. Of course, his words were also a prophecy that Jesus was to die for the nation to redeem them and all humanity from sin and give them eternal life.

Those attending the meeting in Jerusalem did not understand any of that. They thought only in terms of politics and preservation of the status quo. The plot to kill Jesus had taken on an urgency that was missing in the desire to seize him or stone him at the last two festivals. Jesus' time had come. The Passover was near.

Jesus knew what had been decided by the Sanhedrin behind closed doors. Judas became a mercenary part of the plan. But not quite yet. Jesus' time was the Passover in Jerusalem. He and his disciples left Bethany and withdrew across the Jordan back to Perea. This time he sought solitude with his disciples. "Jesus therefore no longer walked openly among the Jews, but went from there to the region near the wilderness, to a town called Ephraim, and there he stayed with the disciples." Somewhere in the wilderness, Jesus sat with his disciples and contemplated what was ahead. He had known from the beginning what must happen.

He had prepared for it, and he spent time preparing his disciples for it too. He had taught them carefully during his entire ministry. In this last year, he had taken special care to be with them. Whenever possible, he had avoided the crowds, especially now in Ephraim. When John mentions the coming of the Passover, he says the time for Jesus was at hand.

Luke tells us that Jesus took his disciples aside and told them exactly what would happen. He includes details he had not spoken of earlier, at least that we know of. We see this with clarity from the perspective after all the events had taken place. They could not have had that perspective. They were totally confused. Six days before the Passover, they were in Bethany. In Bethany, Mary had some inkling of what would happen; she anointed Jesus with oil that she had saved for his burial. But there was still denial. In the garden, Peter tried to defend Jesus with a sword. Then he denied knowing Jesus, and the rest of them ran away in the night and hid. John came to the cross with the Lord's mother, Mary, perhaps out of compassion for the pain she was feeling. None of them had any understanding of what was happening or why.

Jesus knew. He embraced what happened in Jerusalem. He understood that he must take the place of every human. Innocent of sin, he assumed the sin, faults, and imperfections of all humanity and paid the penalty for them all. He was the Messiah, the I AM as he claimed in Jerusalem at the Feast of Booths. True God begotten of the Father and true man born of Mary, his one sacrifice was enough for all sinners everywhere. Because he died and rose again, we are declared just, holy, and innocent and become heirs of heaven. By faith in him we have a place at the feast of the kingdom of God. In Bethany, Jesus prepared for the Passover.

PRAYER: Lord, I am moved by the depth of your love for all of us humans. We are wayward rebels interested only in our own affairs and inflicting deliberate and unintentional harm on others. We deserve to be cast aside and excluded from your love. We cannot do anything to deserve your love. But you love us deeply and gave your life for us. I praise you for your unwarranted love, and I ask you to cause that love to move me in everything I do, say, and think so that I give you glory and honor. For the sake of your glory. Amen.